FROM TRAUMA TO PEACE

How we reclaim our lives

Healing Body and Soul

GERDA C. ROBINSON

"Gerda's life story speaks to the suffering of countless Germans whose lives were tragically traumatized during the Nazi regime. Her unique story also echoes a universal longing for inner peace, a yearning shared by so many in a broken and fearful world. I am deeply moved by Gerda's spiritually and psychologically illuminating journey. I'm sure From Trauma to Peace will bring hope and inspiration to you as it did to me."

—Christopher J. Romig, Senior Pastor, Venice Presbyterian Church, Venice, Florida

"This is a heart-wrenching tale about Gerda and how she survived Nazi Germany. As one of many innocent German children, Gerda's childhood was destroyed, but she wanted to capture her journey to inner peace on paper. Then her story will be complete, and her voice will speak for the children who couldn't."

—Louise Reiter, former editor of The Palm Beach Post and short-story writer

—⁓ﻬﻬ⁓⁓—

"A true and heartbreaking account of an innocent child in Germany during the Nazi dictatorship who spent a lifetime seeking relief from chronic pain resulting from the war."

—Jack Perkins, former US presenter of the
TV program "Biography"

—⁓ﻬﻬ⁓⁓—

"A heartbreaking journey through the horrors of World War II from a child's perspective."

—Dr Christopher Cortman, psychologist and author of
"Your Soul: Instructions for a Better Life"

iii

Acknowledgement

I have received many comments and personal messages from readers of my story. A dear friend, Beth Saurer, sent the following handwritten note to me. I deeply cherish her kind words of love and praise. I was moved after I read her compliments and realized how much I had grown emotionally.

Dearest Gerda,

Thank you so much for sharing this beautiful story of your life. You are the strongest and the most resilient friend I ever had. I am so proud to call you my friend. I can't even imagine the life you led as a child! How did you ever learn to love with what you were living through. You are God's miracle. I cherish your friendship, and I need you to know you are my HERO! None of us will ever really know how you have suffered all those years ago. You are the most compassionate person I know. My heart my love and my caring will be with you every day. I am so blessed to know you

DEDICATION

I'd like to dedicate this book to my siblings, as well as the other children who survived the war. My hope is that this story will bring peace to their souls.

TABLE OF CONTENTS

THOUGHTS OF THE AUTHOR

Because of my childhood history, I feel compassion for the children of today's world. They were exposed to pandemic experiences and many live in families with financial hardships. They, too, were robbed of a carefree, normal childhood.

Teachers could develop a curriculum for social and emotional learning. I just recently heard that the state of New York is one of the progressive states that is already implementing this. Here in Florida, the psychologist Dr. Christ Cortman is working on our school system. Dr. Loran Pilling, my lifesaver and hero, often says we have to help the children express their feelings in words because they haven't yet developed the vocabulary for it. We can create a healthier way of communicating. We should make sure that our children are protected and loved so that they can develop optimally.

INTRODUCTION

I am a survivor of World War II, so this is my story. Not as a persecuted Jew but as an innocent German child. Why tell my story now? There are two reasons.

The time is approaching when my generation will be gone from this earth. I want to be a voice for all the blameless German children who were denied a childhood. The stories are innumerable and simply heartbreaking, and the tragedies of war do not end when the last bomb is dropped, or the last prisoner is freed; they continue, sometimes in subtle but devastating ways. I do not at all minimize the atrocities or the persecution and killing of millions of Jews and others caused by the ruthless power of Nazi Germany. I simply want the reader to understand how the German children suffered.

I also hope that my story can be of help to those who suffer in the aftermath of any kind of trauma. My life's journey has included hunger, fear, and neglect, as well as physical and emotional abuse. I carried these injustices in my mind and body for many years. At various times, I experienced debilitating back pain, headaches, panic attacks, depression, and feelings of inadequacy—all brought on by unexpressed emotions related to my past. One of the important messages of this book is that intense emotions cannot be suppressed forever, and when they're finally released, the process can be as violent and ravaging as an erupting volcano. But after every firestorm, there is a relative calm. Even as my life seemed to lie in shambles, with every raw nerve exposed, I knew that the full expression of my emotions was the single most important thing I could have done for my health and well-being. Only after the release could I begin to pick up the pieces and rebuild my life.

I put the story together bit by bit. Some are my own memories gleaned from the little girl I once was, and some were gathered from the minds of my relatives who lived through it, too. I used historical records, including a few photographs that have endured, to capture certain moments for the reader and to help my family members expand on my life's memories. Although the dialogues are fictional, I believe I've created a fair representation of what each person would probably have said based on their personality and character traits. The names of some persons, in response to their request, have been replaced with pseudonyms.

CHAPTER 1
FIRST, THERE WAS PAIN

The morning of March 15, 1978, was hectic. I plopped scrambled eggs on plates, buttered toast, and poured glasses of orange juice like a veteran short-order cook. I was trying to get my children ready for school, and their plodding pace through the morning ritual was driving me crazy.

"Breakfast is on the table!" I shouted down the hallway, hoping they would hear me as they were getting dressed. "Now!"

Why couldn't they move a little faster? Anxiety knotted my stomach as I thought about what lay in front of me today. I would be checking myself into the Metropolitan Medical Center's pain rehabilitation program. So much was unknown, and I dreaded that.

I turned the tap on at the sink and placed the hot frying pan underneath the running water. The water sizzled as if to empathize with my jangling nerves. Glancing through the kitchen window, I saw an abundance of Minnesota snow. We'll probably get some more, I thought. After six years here, the cold and snow didn't seem to bother me too much anymore. However, I recalled that our first winter was rough. If my husband Dallas had not accepted a transfer with IBM, Minnesota would have remained just a name on a map.

"These eggs are getting cold!" I shouted a second reminder.

"Mom, I'm right here," Kim said, her brother Carl trailing behind.

The photo below, taken during that year, pictures our son

Carl at age nine and our daughter Kim at age eleven. I felt guilty for yelling at them and even guiltier for leaving them. For the next four weeks, my new home would be the chronic pain rehab center.

As they bundled up against the cold to leave for school, I remember how sad they looked. Kim stood quietly by the door, staring at the floor. Carl was silent, too. He never asked any questions—he was such an easygoing child—and he never complained about anything.

I tried to burn an image of them in my brain: blonde bangs framed Kim's cute face. Carl's clothing complemented his stoic demeanor: he had chosen a mature-looking plaid shirt to accompany his jeans. At first, I couldn't look them in the eyes; the guilt I felt about putting too much responsibility on their young shoulders was tremendous. When I hugged them goodbye, my pent-up tears couldn't be restrained any longer.

"I'll call every day," I reminded them.

2

They made their way down the driveway, and before their colorful backpacks bobbed out of sight, I waved, but they didn't see me. Kim reached for Carl's hand. They didn't turn back, and neither would I.

———⟋⟍ooⱺⱺ⟍ooⱺⱺ⟍ooⱺ⟍ⱺⱺ⟍oo⟍⟍———

By definition, chronic pain is long-lasting and unrelenting. Like many people's pains, mine started as something different enough from normal to get my attention: it was tightness in my lower back. Over the weeks and months, it would come and go—sometimes mild and sometimes severe. Eventually, it was so strong that it began to change my life drastically. I couldn't keep up with the housework. Whether I was standing or sitting, the pain never abated. I became lethargic, a ghost of the vibrant and active person I once was. I used to love working in my garden and playing tennis, but not anymore. Our social life trickled down to nonexistence.

At first, my pain was manageable. I convinced myself I could handle anything, including this annoying pain, and I succeeded—for a while. But month after month, the pain got worse. When over-the-counter medicines did little to ease it, I welcomed the relief Valium gave me. At least I could sleep.

When I could no longer deal with the pain on my own, I made an appointment with Dr. John Hartwig, an orthopedic specialist practicing right where we lived in Edina. He ordered a battery of tests—X-rays, myelograms, and discograms—but nothing abnormal showed up. Most of the tests were just tedious, but the discogram was especially traumatic. Needles were inserted into the discs of my spine, which caused unimaginable agony. At that moment, I wished I had a pill to swallow that would end everything.

And although this horrible experience may have ruled out certain conditions that the doctors suspected were causing my

3

pain, it didn't yield a diagnosis.

"Gerda," said Dr. Hartwig with no small hint of frustration, "I wish you had something I could fix."

Dr. Hartwig recommended putting me in a soft body cast. I went along with his suggestion, mainly because he assured me I could remove it for showering and sleeping. For the next four weeks, I was a model patient and meticulously adhered to his instructions. At the follow-up visit a month later, I was disappointed with the results. My pain had not been alleviated at all.

Not willing to perform exploratory surgery on me, Dr. Hartwig suggested a hard body cast. This time, the tight, corset-like cast was extremely uncomfortable and as hard as concrete. Short of having it cut off, there was no way to remove it. The four weeks dragged on at a snail's pace, and in the end, I still had no relief.

Next came a referral to the Mayo Clinic in Rochester, Minnesota. I believed that the facility, with its stellar reputation, might finally see what everyone else had missed and thereby uncover the source of my chronic pain. Tentatively, I regained some of my lost optimism. For such a long time, I had felt useless because I couldn't properly take care of my family or my home. In retrospect, I recognize that I was probably depressed. In fact, I recall thinking that my kind, smart, and handsome husband could find someone much better than me for a wife. Thankfully, Dallas stuck by me.

———◦◦◦◦◦◦◦———

The day we drove to the Mayo Clinic, a blustery wind made the one-and-a-half-hour trip challenging. Dallas had a hard time keeping the car steady on the road. We drove in silence, Dallas focused on his driving and I was too distracted

4

by anxiety to make conversation.

When we arrived, I was still nervous; however, I was determined to undergo the next few hours of testing with an open mind. Two doctors performed the exams, and later, after reviewing my test results and Dr. Hartwig's file, they concurred that there was nothing physically wrong with me. I was stunned!

"Then what is wrong with me?" I asked as a wave of tears began to rise.

"Well," one of the doctors said, "we recommend you see Dr. Loran Pilling. He's a psychiatrist in Minneapolis who runs a chronic pain clinic."

The other doctor added, "We believe this is your best option." What were they trying to tell me—that I was crazy? This was the last thing I ever expected to hear. Angry and perplexed, I spit out my next words. "You want me to see a psychiatrist?" I didn't wait for an answer. I stomped out of the room and didn't care how rude I might have appeared to them.

"You don't need a psychiatrist," Dallas reassured me as he followed me to the car.

The trip home seemed twice as long.

———ᴠᴠᴏᴏᴏᴇᴛᴏᴏᴛᴇᴏᴏᴠᴠ———

The next several weeks were physically and emotionally wrenching. I struggled to grasp the reality that this incessant pain was taking away my ability to be a good wife and mother—the two roles in my life that were most precious to me.

Dallas brought home fast-food hamburgers and buckets of fried chicken so I wouldn't have to cook. Kim was constantly asking me whether there was anything she could do to help.

Carl stared at me as I reclined in bed or on the couch, and I knew he was confused by my lethargy. I couldn't see a way out, and whenever I remembered the doctors' advice at the Mayo Clinic, I would wrestle again with the stigma of seeing a psychiatrist.

I didn't want anybody to think I had a "mental problem." Once labeled this way, I was sure I'd always be known as "that crazy lady." But it has been said that sometimes you have to hit rock bottom before you find your way back up, and after weeks of wallowing in self-doubt and misery, I finally made a decision: I was going to see Dr. Pilling, and I didn't care who knew.

I inhaled a big breath of courage. "I'm going to see Dr. Pilling," I declared, and finally, the decision was out in the open. I searched Dallas's eyes, looking for his reaction. He knew better than to disagree with me after I made up my mind. I was ready to listen to Dr. Pilling's opinions.

———

The day of my appointment finally arrived. I was apprehensive and scared to see a psychiatrist for my physical ailments. I also knew that friends and neighbors were talking about Gerda Robinson, who is going into treatment by a psychiatrist. That stigma was more evident in the '70s than today.

I opened the door, and the waiting time was over. Dr. Pilling stood up and gave me a warm handshake. He was a tall and slender gentleman; his eyes behind the stylish glasses were warm, and his voice put me totally at ease. He sat straight across from me, and after some small talk, his friendly voice came right to the point, and he began to ask me questions. During this first half-hour session, he quizzed me about my life as a child living in Germany. Just before our time was up, he gave me his conclusion.

"Gerda," he said, "I believe your pain stems from your traumatic childhood. You have experienced a lot of fear and sorrow while growing up in Germany during the war." His face softened with compassion. "I believe my clinic can help you. Just let me know when you're ready to start."

"I'll think about it," I said, full of skepticism. After we said our goodbyes, I mulled over my misgivings.

I didn't think this man could help me. How can an unhappy childhood cause back pain? The concept seemed too farfetched to be plausible, and I dismissed it as ridiculous. I was sane and normal, at least on the outside. Even Dallas agreed that Dr. Pilling wouldn't be able to help me.

Days later, reason overtook doubt. Maybe I should give therapy a chance. After all, I had nothing to lose but my pain. Once I had decided on this, I was able to convince my husband that Dr. Pilling's clinic was worth a try.

Armed with a plan, I started organizing my upcoming departure. I prepared lists—lots of them. They were lists of important phone numbers, easy and favorite recipes, and things to do when the freezer needed to be defrosted or when a spot refused to come out of one of Dallas's dress shirts. I even made a list of possible relatives who would be able to care for the children while I was away. Ironically, that list was short.

I thought about my aunt, Tante Erna, who lived in Germany. Although she often told me she'd help in any way she could, there was a language barrier: she couldn't speak English, and Kim and Carl never learned German. The other possible caretaker was Dallas's uncle, Gilbert Robinson. Widowed a few years earlier, he lived alone in St. Louis. When

7

we asked for his help, his enthusiastic response was encouraging despite the fact that he and Aunt Clare had never had any children of their own. To ease our minds, several neighbors agreed to help if Uncle Gilbert needed it. Also, I knew I'd be able to check up on the kids by telephone during my free time at the clinic.

I packed my suitcase and left it by the back door. Dallas would drive me there on his way to work. It was convenient that IBM's office was located in downtown Minneapolis; he would be able to visit me during his lunch break or even after work.

Once again, we traveled in silence. Dallas's face was clouded with concern, although he assured me he had resigned himself to my course of treatment. I, on the other hand, concentrated on what was in store for me at the clinic.

"Can I turn on the radio?" he asked.

"Yes," I said, nodding. It seemed like a good distraction.

The pain clinic loomed ahead. No going back now, I thought. The elevator whisked us to the third floor for check-in. Walking down the hall, I happened to catch an image of myself in a mirror. My reflection was shocking! I wondered, who is this old woman? Sadly, I realized it was me—nobody else could lay claim to that bland beige sweater. Could my apathetic appearance be related to the stress I was feeling inside? What happened to the vivacious and active woman I used to be? I was only forty years old.

Was it that long ago when I used to play competitive tennis, do volunteer work, mow the lawn, and paint the house? Where did all that energy go? I didn't know for sure, but I knew I wanted it back.

I wanted to be in charge of my life, running my household with ease and efficiency. But today, I needed to take the first step toward getting well. Again!

Dr. Pilling and a young man named Denny greeted us. I would find out later that Denny was to be my personal therapist. My internal stress was beginning to show, and I wasn't too steady on my feet. They offered me a chair, and I was grateful to see their eyes brimming with concern.

Dr. Pilling reminded my husband about the twice-weekly evening lectures. All family members were encouraged to attend, and Dallas agreed to be present whenever possible.

"I'll do anything to get my Gerda well again." He gave me a big hug before he left.

As Denny escorted me to my room, I assessed his age to be in the thirties. Although he was thin and small, his kind eyes and gentle demeanor calmed me. I knew I could trust him.

"This is your room," he said, gesturing toward an open door. "There's the bathroom you'll share with Nancy, your neighbor." He gave me directions to my first meeting and left me to unpack.

I glanced around the Spartan-like room. Typical institutional décor—worn linoleum floor; white Venetian blinds lowered to half-mast; and a small, white nightstand beside an iron bed clad with stiff, hospital-cornered sheets. The tiny closet could accommodate the limited wardrobe I brought with me. Peering out the window, I noticed the huge parking lot below. Not a tree was in sight. I sat on the bed, a little lost and uncertain. I felt the plastic mattress cover shifting beneath me, its crinkling sound unfamiliar to my ears.

—wwww⌒◦⌒◦⌒◦⌒◦⌒◦www—

I managed to find the large meeting room, but as I slipped inside, I realized everybody was waiting for me. My face grew red, a beacon of humiliation.

"Gerda," Dr. Pilling said calmly, "we're ready to start. Please have a seat." He pointed to the lone empty spot.

He began his introduction with a reminder about applicable privacy laws, which dictated that we should never talk about patients outside the hospital. I learned that the four-week program consisted of both individual and group sessions with him and the assigned therapist. During my stay, I would learn about relaxation and exercise and be expected to participate in occupational therapy. All of us would be busy for the whole day— except for a lunch and dinner break. I could leave the hospital on Friday afternoons but had to return on Sunday evenings. Listening carefully, I couldn't help but wonder how this program could ease my pain.

Dr. Pilling explained how we would each belong to one of two groups of eight patients. Some patients were in their last week of therapy, others were in their second or third, but the six of us who were new were eager to begin.

I listened as the doctor enlightened us about our feelings and why we needed to express them. "You have to learn to articulate your emotions; it should be as easy and natural as breathing in and out. Don't ignore them." To reinforce how fruitless it was to block out emotion, he added, "Try holding your breath and see how long you can do it." He went on to say how stifled emotions could cause all kinds of illnesses. "But more of that later," he promised. By then, my first day at the clinic was half over. It was lunchtime, and all sixteen patients headed toward the elevators. Being so new, I just followed the others. Inside, I felt awkward and lost, especially when the crowd broke up into groups of three or four people, bonding with each other almost immediately. I made sure I smiled if anyone looked my way; I wanted to get absorbed into one of the groups as quickly as possible. The elevator arrived and opened its doors with a lively ding. Everyone rushed in, afraid to be left alone. With a second to spare, someone grabbed my hand and pulled me into the comfort of the crowd. I turned my head to acknowledge my savior.

"My name's Nancy," she said when her delicate hand took mine. "Gerda," I responded, grasping the lifeline that her fingers offered.

"You and I are neighbors… we share the bathroom between our rooms. I'm a bit meticulous, but I know we'll get along fine. By the way, my husband claims I snore," Nancy said, shaking her head to demonstrate she thought otherwise, "so I won't be offended if you close both doors."

I shared a table with my newfound friend while we ate our lunch of bland meatloaf, instant mashed potatoes, and overcooked green beans. The lime Jell-O was pretty good, though. After lunch, the day continued with exercise and relaxation sessions. The idea of making time for myself every day was strange. Besides, my body hurt too much to do the exercises.

"You can do it, Gerda; I know you can." Nancy flashed a big smile at me. With her encouragement, I finished the exercises. To this day, I still do them. If I try to shirk my routine, Nancy's face pops into my head, and she prods me with those words.

Next came the relaxation session. I liked it the best. After we got comfortable lying down on the mat, we listened to soothing sounds like the ocean's waves washing over the shore or birds twittering their happy songs in the trees. Along with the resonance of the background noise, a calm and gentle voice on the tape recorder reminded us what a special place this was, a place where we could unload our problems.

I realized Denny's soothing voice was on the tape, and I almost fell asleep.

When the session was finished, Denny—the real one— explained how we could expect a good night's sleep after listening to the tapes. "Remember," he said, "your bodies can go to sleep now because they are calm—no more taking the daily problems to bed."

One of my group members, a bear of a man named George, had a brilliant smile. His bright blue shirt prompted me to say, "You must feel pretty perky wearing that shirt."

"No, ma'am," he said, "I wear these bright colors to cheer myself up." Then, he told me about the injuries he sustained while working at a construction site. Although he recovered from the physical wounds, he still experienced pain. "The doctors can't see anything on my X-rays, so they tell me it must be in my head." He tapped his temple with his right index finger. "All I know is I'm in constant pain." He didn't have a good night's sleep until he came to the clinic. "After I listen to those tapes, I sleep like a baby!"

His enthusiasm gave me hope. Maybe the relaxation tapes would work for me, too.

On my first night at the hospital, I talked to my husband and the kids. I tried to concentrate on their words, but my mind wandered through the day's activities. The strange surroundings closed in on me. I cut my conversation short, took a Valium, and let it lull me to sleep.

———⟋⟍⟋⟍∘⟍∘⟋⟍⟋⟍∘∘⟋⟍⟋⟍———

A loud, strange noise, like a car hitting a tree, abruptly

woke me up from my sound slumber. I may have dreamed it, but it seemed real enough to propel me from the bed. The shock of the cold linoleum on my bare feet made me twist my back, and I was painfully reminded why I was there in the first place.

Actually, I was glad to be awake—anything to stop the nightmares. I'd been having them since I was a child in Germany, and they were vivid, terrifying, and unforgettable. One of the dreams took place in the apartment where we lived during the war. It was up one floor in a five-family building. The main front door downstairs had to be locked at ten o'clock every night. Even though I was the youngest girl in the family, my mother often relegated this chore to me. In the dream, I'm walking down the steps, and just before I can turn the key, a scary, scar-faced man pulls me down the nearby basement stairs. When I scream with terror, I wake up.

It was bad enough that I had these nightmares repeatedly as a child, but the worst part was not having anybody to comfort me. I had been alone in my misery.

———⁓⁓∾⊙⊱⊙⊰⊙∾⊶⁓⁓———

The next morning, while I finished dressing, Denny yelled down the corridor, "Gerda, are you ready for breakfast?"

I must have poked around too much because when I left my room, the halls were empty. Not a soul anywhere. I forgot how to get to the dining room! I panicked for a moment, but after a few wrong turns, I managed to find my destination. I would soon find out that the staff treated all the patients this way. They wanted us to be responsible for ourselves. It was my job to get to breakfast. If I didn't come with the group, I had to figure out a way to get there by myself.

After eating a bowl of cereal and a banana, I went to my

first group session. Dr. Pilling introduced his wife, Carol, a frail-looking brunette wearing a fashionable suit. I was transfixed by her speech.

"I once was a professional ice skater," she began, "until I had taken one too many falls. The accumulated injuries resulted in chronic pain, and I couldn't stand long enough to butter a piece of toast." The sad memory flickered in her eyes. "I was devastated that I had to give up my career and could no longer take care of my family." Captivated by Carol's story, I empathized with her troubles, and for the first time, I felt a glimmer of hope. Her inspiration started in that room, but it continues to this day.

Later that day, Denny led a session for new patients. I learned he was an excellent listener and never tired of our questions. The activity for that meeting was simple: pick a partner, have one lie on the floor with their eyes closed, and talk for five minutes about a predetermined topic. The other person would sit close by and listen. The partner I chose was Debbie—a forty-year-old doctor's wife—who was dependent on Valium and pain pills following a bout of pneumonia. The illness had left her with chronic pain. I opted to lie down and talk first. Denny's assigned topic that day was "What do you remember from when you were five years old?"

I talked about what it was like to grow up in Germany during the war and my best friend, Rosie Oetken. She was a pretty girl with a dimpled smile. Rosie had many dresses because her mother was a seamstress. I was somewhat envious of her wardrobe; mine consisted of shabby hand-me-downs. Sometimes, I felt too embarrassed to be seen with her as we walked to school. My envy didn't stop with her new outfits. I wanted my mother to lavish attention on me like Rosie's mom did for her. Every morning, her mother waved goodbye to her when she left for school. My mother never waved. She was too depressed because she couldn't feed us. Most of the time, our cupboards were bare, and all of us kids had to fend for ourselves.

If we managed to scrounge up a piece of dry bread, it was our breakfast.

As I continued talking about my depressed mother, Debbie became a little agitated.

"Gerda, stop crying; I can't understand you," she pleaded.

It was true. I was blubbering like a baby. For many years, I had suppressed the fear, anger, sadness, and confusion of this formative period in my life.

"I'm so sorry you had such a rotten childhood," Debbie said, tears in her eyes. "That must have been awful for you."

It was the first time I had confronted my past. I had traveled three thousand miles alone to forget that godforsaken, miserable country, but now I realized I had to unlock the horrible memories and come to terms with them. I had taken the first step. Could I gather the courage to take the next one?

CHAPTER 2
IT'S ALL ABOUT SURVIVAL

In another recurring nightmare that began in childhood, I am walking down the street when I suddenly lose my footing and fall over a steep cliff. My body catches on some branches, and I am staring down a bottomless abyss. It's at this point that I always wake up. As long as I know when to stop watching this little internal movie, I will never fall, and I will never have to learn what's at the bottom of the dark hole. In many ways, this has been an apt metaphor for my life.

I took my first breath on October 7, 1938. I'd like to believe that someone was happy when I was born, but that illusion died with many of my other naïve notions a long time ago. The precise time of my birth is unknown, but I have been told that I came out screaming. Maybe I could sense that my life was going to be a rollercoaster ride, and I wanted to stay in my protective cocoon just a little longer. Never again would I be so warm and secure.

My birthplace was a town called Bad Charlottenbrunn, nestled in the serene Riesengebirge (Sudeten Mountains) of eastern Germany, in a region called Schlesien. The nearest large city was Breslau, about 50 miles away. Poland took possession of most of Schlesien after the Second World War. However, at the time of my birth, no one would have imagined such a thing was possible.

People flocked to Bad Charlottenbrunn to recuperate from serious illnesses. The notable spa town was a peaceful haven for those seeking its healing attributes. The men who lived there worked either in the coal mines or in the local porcelain factory. The women stayed home, cooked meals, and raised the children.

In 1933, my nineteen-year-old mother, Gertrud Gaertner, and my twenty-three-year-old father, Fritz Hartwich, were married. (They're pictured here on his favorite form of transportation.)

A year later, their first daughter, Ilse, was born. Two and a half years after that, a second daughter arrived. Although she was named Edeltraut, everybody called her Traute for short. I came into the world about a year later. Within five short years, the Hartwich family had increased from two to five. We weren't desperately poor—we lived in an apartment with the basics of family life—but I often wonder whether my parents were happy during those early years. Maybe they were too busy raising three small children to think about such an abstract concept as happiness.

Like most people, I have only sparse memories of my early childhood. I had to glean the forgotten details by talking with my aunt in later years and poring over family photos. This is what I know about my mother—she was a slim, 110-pound woman with dark blonde hair and blue eyes. Her hair was naturally curly and cut short, which softened her features. Although she didn't fit the image of classical beauty, she was certainly nice-looking. Kind by nature, my mother wasn't prone to gossip like many others were in her small town. Her biggest flaw, in the eyes of her in-laws, was that she came from a poor family. Fritz's parents and sister believed he had chosen the wrong wife, and they showed her no respect. Perhaps that's why, in the old photos, there always seems to be a hint of sadness around her eyes.

My father was also small in stature, with deep-set, steel-blue eyes and a rather prominent nose. Restless by nature, he seemed constantly searching for work and often accepted jobs that would take him out of town for a week or more. As a self-taught musician, he played the trumpet in a circus band. He also took advantage of opportunities in the local employment sector by working in the mines or the factory. I think he was happiest when he could get away, as it was easier than to avoid his part of the responsibility for raising three girls. In fact, even when he was there, he wasn't much help at all.

Around this time, Hitler's popularity was on the rise, especially in the cities. More and more, Germans were praising him as a powerful speaker, and they wanted to believe him when he promised to reopen the factories and rebuild the roads. He gave the people hope for a new beginning. However, my parents' interest in politics was minimal, and the radio broadcasts and newspapers that hinted at Hitler's increasing support would have held no significance for them.

The photo below shows my father's parents on the left, their daughter Erna in the middle, and their two boys, Robert (rear) and Fritz (front).

My father's sister, my Tante Erna, was the delight of her parents. She was a talented woman who could cook and sew like a professional. These talents allowed her to make extra money outside the house. She managed her household budget well enough to invite her mother (my grandmother) to live with her and her husband Wilhelm—also known as "Willie"— after her father (my grandfather) died of cancer.

Onkel Willie was a wonderful Mensch. I never met him, but everyone said he was a true "family man" in the best sense of that expression. He wasn't just a hard worker who would take any job to put food on the table; he also took a real interest in playing with his daughter, and he had a beautiful relationship with my aunt, who worshipped the ground he walked on. Even my grandparents loved him more than they did their own son—my father, Fritz.

Tante Erna and Onkel Willie had two children, Klaus and Inge, who were six and three, respectively, at the time of my birth in 1938. Erna's extra income and my uncle's salary from his job at the porcelain factory allowed them to live comfortably.

I never knew my paternal grandfather because he died when I was quite young. I learned he was a community leader and a foreman for the coal miners. My aunt liked to tell a funny story about his prized possession—a bicycle. Apparently, he was so particular about maintaining its pristine condition that he would pick it up and carry it across a puddle rather than ride through the water. In the winter, he would take it apart to clean it and then hang up each part to dry thoroughly.

These few details about my earliest family life are all that I've been able to gather over the years. It's not much—not much at all.

⸻⁓⁓∿◦◦✕◦✕◦∿∿⁓⸻

Politics could no longer be ignored as Hitler was becoming more powerful. The rumor of impending war filled the airwaves and the newspapers, and the course of my life would soon change drastically.

Because I was so little—an infant at best—I may not be so accurate with my dates. I've tried to piece together events from the faded memories of my relatives. I was probably about a year old when my father announced that Hitler's army had drafted him and he would be sent to Wilhelmshaven, which is located by the North Sea.

Fear seeped into the homes and people of Bad Charlottenbrunn as the men left for active duty. The reality of the war, now underway, terrified the once-sleepy town. Women dressed in funeral colors and betraying their dread that loved ones would never come home.

My mother panicked when she realized she would have to leave the comfort of the only home she had ever known. She didn't even know where Wilhelmshaven was, but my father had been called to serve in the armed forces, so she had no choice but to go. The plan was that my father would go first so he could secure living quarters. A few weeks later, he sent a telegram confirming that he had rented an apartment and wanted us to join him.

I was too little to travel, especially during the uncertainties and dangers of the war. My grandmother and aunt convinced my mother to leave me behind in their care. The two strong-willed women intimidated my mother easily. With her meek demeanor, she probably acquiesced without much of a struggle. That's how I first became separated from my mother and my sisters.

About a week after my father's telegram arrived, my mother, Ilse, and Traute left for Wilhelmshaven. My aunt recalled the departure as stiff and unemotional. No one hugged, no one cried. There were a few stoic handshakes, and then my loved ones were gone. I would not see them for another three years. I often wonder whether this early separation and lack of playtime together could explain our later difficulty in bonding.

———❧———

My father sent Tante Erna a letter to announce the safe arrival of his wife and children. He also mentioned they were settling in well among the 100,000 other inhabitants of Wilhelmshaven. The town had a huge shipyard that manufactured and repaired submarines and other ships. The service trained my father as a welder, and his contribution to the war effort at that time was helping build these vessels.

Back in Bad Charlottenbrunn, Tante Erna struggled to provide for her two children—Klaus and Inge—and me, as well as her mother. She missed the support of her loving Willie, who had been drafted into Hitler's army. The fact that Willie had children didn't seem to matter. He didn't dare ignore the draft; everybody who refused disappeared forever. The common thread among women was fear for the lives of their husbands and sons. They all waited anxiously for the mailman to arrive. At first, Onkel Willie's letters came on a regular basis, but after a short while, they stopped.

One day, Tante Erna received a telegram. Fear gripped her heart as she gathered us all around the table so she could open the dreaded yellow envelope. It stated that Wilhelm Fiedler was missing in action. Distraught, my aunt screamed, "Oh, no! Not my Willie!" Klaus, Inge and I stared at each other. Although my aunt had a terrible burden to bear, she had to be strong to protect those in her care. Her mother, her two children, and I depended on her.

———⟋⟍⟋⟍∘◠◯↝◯◯↝◯∘◠⟍⟍———

One day after Tante Erna returned from the market, she said, "Can you believe the grocery store has no meat?" She was frantic at the thought of going hungry. "They didn't even have any more fruit or vegetables," she said, still trying to come to grips with the reality of it.

The scarcity of food was another reminder of the ongoing war. More often than not, the women of the town wore frightened looks on their faces, especially when the shopkeepers had to tell their customers, "Come back tomorrow; I might get a delivery." Everyone was scared of the uncertain future. We all wondered whether we would have enough food for another meal—or would this one be the last?

Another constant concern was medical care. Everyone

prayed to stay healthy, but in 1940, my five-year-old cousin Inge became quite ill. My aunt fretted for a few days as Inge refused to eat and had a fever. Finally, Tante Erna took her child to see the family doctor. To her surprise, the doctor had been replaced by one who was in the Schutzstaffel, which translates as "Protection Squadron," but is better known as the SS, a military force of the Nazi Party. This was my aunt's first encounter with the infamous SS. She later learned that her own family doctor, a kind and wonderful man, had married a woman whose grandparents were Jewish. He and his family disappeared and were never heard from again.

The SS doctor diagnosed Inge with influenza, and he told my aunt to keep her in bed and give her aspirin. Inge grew more listless. She didn't want to play with me anymore, nor would she allow anyone in her room. After several days, my aunt took her ill child back to the SS doctor. Again, the instructions were to keep her in bed and give her aspirin.

When a neighbor stopped in a couple of days later, she implored my aunt, "For goodness' sake, take the child to the hospital—she's dying!"

Tante Erna carried her daughter's frail body to the hospital. Inge didn't have the flu; she had diphtheria, a serious childhood disease back then. But it was too late. Inge was too weak to recover, and she died. Years later, when my aunt told me the story, she said that Inge had stood up in her hospital bed, raised her arms, and said, "I want to go home, Mommy." At the time, she had reassured her little girl that she would be going home soon. Years later, as a born-again Christian, my aunt now believes that her daughter was referring to the "heavenly home."

Either way, the child's passing devastated Erna, especially because the wrong diagnosis caused a needless death. My aunt told me that if she could have closed her eyes and died herself, she gladly would have done so. The loss of her child was surely the most difficult burden she ever faced.

In spite of her pain—or maybe because of it—Tante Erna resolved to be strong. She still had Klaus, her mother, and me to care for; we needed her desperately. Because my own wardrobe was so meager, Tante Erna dressed me in her deceased daughter's clothes. Only as an adult did I realize what an act of kindness that was and how utterly painful it must have been for her.

———$\sim\!\!\!\text{mod}\text{ex}\text{ore}\text{om}\!\!\!\sim$———

Losing her daughter was almost unbearable, but Tante Erna tried her best to cheer us up. She made an extra effort to get milk and eggs from the kind people who rented us their apartment. These ingredients were often used to make pancakes; believe it or not, I got so tired of eating them! To get me to force another forkful down my throat, my aunt had to bribe me with a piece of jellied candy. "Take another bite, Gerda," she would plead with me, "and I'll give you a piece of candy." Since chocolate or any kind of candy was almost nonexistent, I choked down that last bite to get a sweet treat.

Food was scarce, but we scraped by. I don't remember having any toys or books. The town was so small that there wasn't much to do, even when we had free time. To top it off, I was constantly frightened by the turkeys that ran on the farm next to Tante Erna's place. I distinctly remember wearing a red dress one day, which must have incited them to chase me. I screamed in terror and ran to the outdoor potty, standing on the shelf and bellowing for someone to save me.

I can't say that all my memories from that time are bad, though. I fondly recall going blueberry picking with my aunt in the hills behind our apartment building and sledging down those same hills in wintertime. I was lucky to be alive, and for the most part, I was healthy. But in 1942, when I was four, I contracted diphtheria. The only cure at the time was to get a blood transfusion, and the blood had to come from my parents. My father was stationed in France; my mother was in Wilhelmshaven. Both had to travel a great distance, but travel they did. Coincidentally, they were on the same train for many hours but were unaware of each other's presence. I don't remember how I felt about seeing them again; after all, I was only four. But our family, true to the German stereotype, was more inclined to be stoic than affectionate, so I imagine the whole thing must have been treated as a practical matter that simply needed tending to.

After I received the transfusion, my health returned. My father immediately traveled back to France, but my mother stayed with me at Tante Erna's house until she was sure I had recuperated enough to return to Wilhelmshaven with her. As our departure date loomed closer, conflicting emotions tugged me in two directions. I was glad at the prospect of being reunited with my sisters, whom I hadn't seen in three years, but I was sad to leave Tante Erna's care.

The train ride to Wilhelmshaven was horrible. We had to wait for hours for the train to arrive, and when it did, there was such chaos of people pushing and shoving that I ended up being separated from my mother. The station suddenly looked so big and frightening, with everyone rushing in different directions and the sounds of squealing brakes and steam escaping as the trains barreled in and out on a maze of tracks. I was frantic. "Mama, Mama, where are you?" I screamed in desperation. Finally, an older man realized my plight and reunited me with my mother. He had to lift me up from the station's platform and pass me through the train window into her arms. I can only imagine how relieved my mother must have been.

The train was jammed with people. We were lucky to find a seat, and perched on my mother's lap, I finally fell asleep. Several hours later, I woke up hungry and thirsty. We would have to change trains in Hamburg, and knowing my mother was a woman who was shy, introverted, and unsure of herself, I'm certain that the whole journey must have been overwhelming for her. We got off the train, and my mother repeatedly asked people around her whether we were on the right platform for Wilhelmshaven. Air raid sirens screamed in the distance. Germany was under regular attack by then, but it was the first time I had heard this sound, and I was frightened. Planes flew low overhead, people screamed, and my mother held me so tight I could barely breathe. Somehow, we made it to the next train. We arrived in Wilhelmshaven ten hours later than scheduled.

When we got home, Ilse and Traute were ecstatic to see me. "Look how much you've grown!" they both said. Ilse picked me up and twirled me around. She almost dropped me. Then we girls hugged each other, happy to be reunited. I noticed how skinny and pale my sisters looked. "Don't worry," Traute said, a reassuring smile on her face, "we'll find food somewhere."

Hanna Vasserlovsky had watched my sisters while my mother was away. "I'm so grateful you could look after my children," my mother said, thanking her neighbor. "If I could give you something for your kindness, I would." I believe she gave Mrs. Vasserlovsky a hug instead. Maybe the hardship of war was at least making it easier for us to get a little closer to one another.

"Gertrud, my dear friend, I'm glad I could help you," Hanna said, beaming. Even though she was dressed shabbily, the twinkle in her eye and her pleasant demeanor were infectious—we felt happy, peaceful, and contented for the moment.

After Mrs. Martin, I glanced around my new home. Our apartment was on the first floor. It had a living room, two bedrooms, a bathroom, and a small kitchen. Some of the furniture was given to us, and some was bought at a second-hand store. Although the rooms were small and the place had no central heating or hot water, it felt cozy.

Families banded together and contracted a coal distributor to deliver one hundred pounds of coal at a time. Kindling wood and newspapers were needed to light the stoves, so it was a bit of a chore to cook, heat the house, and take baths in warm water.

There were five apartments in the building. The attic was used to hang laundry during the winter and rainy seasons. In the basement, we had a small storage locker and a laundry room, which all five families shared. A huge black kettle had to be filled with water and heated with coal or wood to bring the wash to a boil.

Despite our home's bleak surroundings, we were glad to be together again. My older sister, Ilse, was sweet, helpful, and kind. Although she was skinny and pale, her blue eyes sparkled, and her platinum-blonde hair shone. Traute, just a year older than I, had soft brown eyes and an adorable face, although she was thin too. She had a lively spirit and a knack for making us laugh in spite of our troubles.

I didn't like the weather very much in my new hometown. It was depressing. It rained for days, which was not unusual for that part of Germany. The dampness and overcast skies were a dismal complement to the hunger in our bellies. Often, when our cupboards were bare, Frau Vasserlovsky gave us some soup and a few slices of bread. As food became scarcer, ration cards were issued to distribute the insufficient supply equitably. Sometimes, we traded them in for money to buy other essentials, such as shoes or clothing.

There was something else about Wilhelmshaven that made it a less-than-ideal place to live: it was a prime target for Allied bombings. Because it was a major shipyard responsible for building and maintaining U-boats, the town was the object of many air raids. In fact, by the end of the war, half of the city would be destroyed.

In retrospect, it is nothing short of amazing what people— even young children—can adapt to. The bombings were so frequent that I quickly learned the routine: as soon as the air raid sirens sounded, we turned on the radio to get an estimate of when the bombings would start.

I remember my mother yelling, "Hurry up!" as we scrambled to the bomb shelter, which was about ten minutes away on foot. The air raids happened day and night. We usually slept in our clothes so we'd be ready to run in the dark. In our haste, we didn't take anything with us. To amuse ourselves during the long wait until we could return home, we children would play "Ringlein, Ringlein, Du must reisen" (Little ring, little ring, you must wander), a game in which a ring or other small object would be passed secretly from one player to another, and each would have to guess who was holding it.

The bomb shelter was an enormous cylinder-shaped concrete structure, five or six stories tall, with walls four feet thick. Many such shelters were scattered throughout the city, and they were fairly generic. They didn't have windows (for obvious reasons). A spiral staircase wound around the inside walls, and concrete benches lined the perimeter of each floor.

The older people claimed the lower-level seats while the children had to climb the stairs. I suppose that was fair.

Sometimes, we were stuck in the shelter for hours without any food or water. Often, we shivered from hunger as much as from the cold. At least we could huddle together for warmth. What a relief it was when the all-clear siren sounded, and we could go home. I didn't realize it at the time, but the sound of the sirens would plague me for years.

My mother showed signs of failing. She was tired and depressed all the time. Some days, she would stay in bed, and we had to fend for ourselves. Often, we had to go from door to door and beg for a slice of bread. Thankfully, the neighbors who recognized us would give us any food they could spare.

Still, the lack of nutrition was taking its toll on our bodies. I often fainted. I'm sure it was because I was so hungry, but I was never examined by a doctor to confirm this. If my eyes started to roll back in my head, I knew I'd be passing out soon. Sometimes, Ilse saw someone called "Death" playing a violin in the hallway; she asked us if we saw him, too. My fainting spells continued, and my nightmares worsened. But none of this mattered. Nobody was there to listen to my troubles; everyone had troubles of their own. Unbeknownst to me, the layers of repressed emotion were already being formed.

The fragile health of my sister and me drove my mother deeper into depression. Occasionally, when the air raid sirens screamed in the night, my mother would refuse to go to the shelter. Instead, she sat in her bed, staring at the wall. She would send us to the shelter, and although we didn't want to leave her alone, she wouldn't budge.

I suppose there were times she simply didn't care whether she lived or died.

Other times, she regained a little of her will to live and actively pursued the safety of the shelters. Once, after the radio announcer had predicted a heavy attack, Mother led the way with the sirens blaring in the night. When we got to the shelter, it was full. We had to turn around and go home. I remember my mother yelling at us to run faster, faster! I tripped over my shoelaces. "They are right behind us!" Mother screamed, but I couldn't go any faster.

The planes roaring in the distance got louder. "Hurry, hurry!" Mother spurred us on. When we were almost there, we finally recognized our house—they all tended to look the same in the oppressive darkness. We scrambled to the basement, surprised to find some of our neighbors already there. Ilse turned on the light for a moment just to get us oriented. "Turn off the light, you stupid girl!" someone yelled. In the pitch black, we nervously inhaled dust and dampness, the roar of the death-laden airplanes overhead. That night, we were beyond the reach of the planes' destruction. Our lives were spared—again. The all-clear siren sounded its paradoxically mournful cry, and we slipped beneath our covers, fully clothed, until the next siren would rouse our shivering bodies again.

Considering the number of bombs that fell, it is something of a miracle that our apartment was never hit directly. The closest call was when we had gone to the basement for shelter and heard a bomber directly overhead. When we came back up to our apartment, one of our neighbors found a hole in the ceiling and a place on their kitchen table that had been burned.

As the air raids became more frequent, transportation and commercial supply sources were disrupted. The stores were unable to stock clothing, shoes, or food as more and more of the country's resources were devoted to the war. When it was really cold, we didn't venture outside; our shoes were too worn out to provide any protection. My thin coat offered no warmth, even when I wore it to bed. My sisters moved my bed away from the wall because I was so preoccupied with scraping the ice from it that I wasn't getting any sleep. I hardly ever remember looking out the windows during wintertime; they were too thickly cloaked with frost to allow a clear view of what was outside. Occasionally, I would breathe on the opaque windowpane and melt a little hole in the frost. Then, I'd be able to take a peek at the glum world. I couldn't decide what was worse: the hunger, the cold, or the ceaseless howling of the sirens.

True to a child's inherently optimistic spirit, Ilse and I made the best of a bad situation. After the air raids, we would collect pieces of shrapnel. These tidbits of leftover destruction, sometimes still warm from the explosion, would serve as horseshoes. We would compete for hours on end to see who could throw them closer to a target.

I also remember a time when coal was scarce. Once, the kindly distributor man told my mother that he could only offer her a big tree root—but she'd have to split it herself. She was too weak to wield an ax, and no strapping men were around to help. We, kids, scrounged around the neighborhood for anything to burn. Ilse saw a neighbor stealing pieces of a park bench for fuel; if she had gotten there first, we could have stopped looking. Instead, we asked our mother if we could chop up an old wooden chair that sat in the corner of the living room. "Go ahead," she said. Her small face held despondent eyes, but she knew the winter was almost over. As the days got a little longer and warmer, my mother focused on finding seeds so we could plant them. Maybe spring would be kinder.

———⁓⁓∘⊙⊙↹⊙∘⁓⁓———

Weeks grew into months. The air raids became less frequent, but hunger and exhaustion were our constant companions. Once, after looking around for something to eat and finding nothing, Ilse, Traute, and I were so hungry that we decided to make a concoction of vinegar and fake coffee grounds. These were the only two items in the pantry. It tasted awful. We spit out the foul mixture and rinsed our mouths with water. Since it was summer, we decided to take our quest for food outside. We came upon a patch of scratchy thistles, picked them, and brought them home. We cooked our "spinach"—at least that's what we pretended it was—in water, added a little salt, and ate it. It was barely edible, and it didn't taste like spinach at all. At least our stomachs stopped growling for a while.

Even when the threat of being bombed to death had abated somewhat, we still feared for our lives. The rumor floating around was that the dikes by the North Sea were going to be dynamited, thus slowing the Allied troops' advance from the west. We were only ten minutes away from the dikes. While some of our neighbors loaded carts and walked farther south to get some distance between them and the floodwaters, my mother refused to leave. "If we're going to die," she said, "it might as well be in our own home." The dynamite rumor fizzled out; a week or two later, those who left had returned.

Again, the months sped by. The end of the war must have been in sight because there was little left of our city to destroy. That's when the announcement came about the heaviest attack yet. Storeowners were advised to unload all of their food and canned goods and give them away to the townspeople. It was better to let someone eat it rather than destroy it. If people had wagons, they loaded them up with staples. Ilse and I went home with a pillowcase full of sugar and flour and several pounds of butter. I didn't know what we were going to do about the butter because we had no refrigerator. In cold weather, butter and milk could be kept on a shelf built outside a window.

Naturally, after the heavy air raids, food was scarcer. The neighborhood grocery store opened only after it had received a shipment of flour. One time, when the store was open, my mother sent Ilse and me to get a loaf of bread. We took turns standing in line because you had to get there early, sometimes as early as six o'clock the night before. My sister took the first turn, and we alternated four-hour shifts. For twelve hours, we waited in that line, and our biggest fear was that they'd run out before we got our bread. Our stomachs growled, and we became weary of the waiting. But we also knew we would have trouble sleeping if we didn't get anything to eat. Thankfully, on that particular day, we were rewarded with a loaf that was still warm from the oven, and the fresh-baked smell tempted me to eat the whole thing. But I didn't. After it was gone, the laborious process started all over again.

Herr and Frau Meyer lived across the hall from us with their daughter Brigitte. Frau Meyer was obese—a puzzling state to be in when everyone else was starving to death. Later on, I found out that she was quite adept at begging for food from the farmers. Frau Meyer rarely came bicycling home from the country without a full basket of goods.

Herr Meyer liked to drink. We watched him ride away on his bicycle in the morning, but if he were drunk, he'd have to have a horse and carriage bring him home. At first, my crazy neighbors were a little frightening, but after a while, I just ignored them.

With spring in full force, our neighbors' gardens started yielding some produce. Here, we found the perfect opportunity to steal carrots, rutabagas, beans, or cucumbers. In the evenings, the three of us girls sneaked out of the apartment with a flashlight and gathered apples or pears. We didn't feel good about taking other people's harvest, but our hunger drove us to this solution when we couldn't find another way to feed ourselves.

We even managed to have a little fun once in a while. We made up games, one of which involved digging a hole in the ground. Then, armed with five marbles apiece, we flicked the glass orbs into the hole with our forefingers. The one who got all five marbles in the hole with the fewest turns was declared the winner. We also played something we called brennball (burning ball). We used a stick, not a bat, to hit the ball while another player ran around three stops. It was similar to baseball, but I never figured out why it was called brennball. Perhaps the name derived from the stinging or burning sensation we felt in our hands when we caught the ball. When we played these rudimentary games, we were able to forget how difficult life was—at least for a couple of hours.

———

I can't remember the exact date, but I know our father must have come home on leave at least once because along came our baby brother Guenter in 1943. Although our father was supposed to send home money, he didn't—at least not regularly. One day, I discovered why: he had bought himself a motorcycle. When he drove that sleek two-wheeler into the neighborhood, all the children gathered around to touch it and maybe even get a chance to sit on it. It was quite an expensive present he had given himself, and it irked me to hear him brag about how much fun it was to ride. I suspect that a Fräulein or two had ridden on it as well. The gleaming motorcycle might have elevated our status for a few days, but I would rather have had the food and clothes instead.

In the photo below, I was perched on the seat when I was

34

about six years old in a photo op with my sisters.

When his leave was up, my father was sent to the Russian front. He parked the motorcycle in the basement, and it was the only sign of him for years after that. The more I looked at it, unused and gathering dust, the more I thought, "Why don't we sell it?" We girls would talk about that, but we had learned early in life that children had no business expressing their opinions to adults, so we kept it among ourselves.

Although my father would never have qualified for Parent of the Year, I do have at least one happy memory of him. During a period when he was working in a China factory, he made a complete set of twelve place settings for his mother. She treasured it and displayed it attractively on a corner shelf. She enjoyed using the dishes for special occasions.

There is a story about the dishes that I often heard many years later. One day, my grandmother and Tante Erna were looking out the window and saw some soldiers coming toward their house. They knew right away that they were Russian soldiers and that they would take anything of value that they might find. Without knocking on the door, they simply stepped right into the house, and one of them dismissed us with a finger pointing toward the door.

"You have five minutes to collect your belongings!" he declared.

My grandmother and aunt were startled, but they immediately realized that they had better obey. Both women laid several dresses on top of each other for ease of carrying and then collected some small pieces of jewelry and pictures. Then my grandmother looked at her china and her crystal glasses. Gathering all her strength and determination, she took each glass and each piece of china—save two—and smashed it to the floor. She stashed the little sugar bowl and creamer in her coat pocket. She later transferred them into her feather bed, which she also was able to salvage.

The following photo shows the creamer and sugar bowl hand-made by my father. It ended up in my household. The handle of the sugar bowl is now broken, and it reminds me of my fractured relationship with my father.

Whenever I visit other people's homes, see precious family heirlooms displayed, and hear loving memories exchanged, I feel sad. Then I remind myself, "I have a creamer and a broken-handled sugar bowl that my father made in Schlesien. Like me, it's had a difficult journey, but now it's at peace."

———⟋⟍∘∿∘∿∘∿⟍⟋———

Ilse attends school now. She said she liked it, and if you asked her why, the answer was simple: "I get food." It was just a bit of milk and some bread, but I could see how these small morsels would be enough to make me like school, too.

Traute and I had to help with our new baby brother. The added sibling caused our neighbors to wonder whether my mother could care for us, but they had no idea what my mother was capable of.

The motorcycle disappeared from the basement. Soon after, some things materialized in our house that we rarely got to see: a sack of potatoes, a chicken, and some pork. My mother sliced up some of the pork, put it in a pan, and fried it with some onions. With great anticipation, Ilse, Traute, and I stood in silence, inhaling the glorious smells. We hadn't had meat in such a long time that we could hardly wait for our first chance to eat bacon again. It was a meal that has stuck in our minds forever. For the first time in years, our stomachs were full enough to feel satiated. By saving the fat to use like butter and making sandwiches with it, my mother extended the pleasure of this meal as long as possible. When I thought about it later, I reasoned that she must have had some contact with farmers before and knew that she could make a good trade, exchanging the unused motorcycle—and all the painful memories it represented—for something that could contribute positively to our welfare.

———୴୴୦୶ଚ୧ଚ୫ଚ୧ଚ୰ଚ୴୴———

In 1944, when I was six, I started kindergarten. I was thrilled because I was able to eat more regularly. The school day started at 8 a.m., and we had our first break at 10. I watched how the other kids took out their small packages wrapped in brown paper, unfolding the bundles to reveal sandwiches of marmalade or liverwurst they had brought from home. I made a point of going to the bathroom to wait until that break was over because I had nothing to eat. Two hours later, we had another break, during which the school provided soup and milk. I was happy for the soup but couldn't stand the thought of drinking milk.

The teacher sized me up and said, "Gerda, you look thin and pale. You need to drink your milk." I tried to drink it, but I would always start vomiting. I could not get it down through my throat. Nevertheless, I was told I could not get up until I finished it. Sometimes, it would take an hour or more. One day, I was so desperate to escape this unpleasantness that I asked the teacher, "May I have some chocolate milk?" Sometimes, I got lucky, and my request was granted. On those days, the milk went down a lot easier.

I had to remember to raise my right arm and shout, "Heil Hitler!" when I entered the classroom or greeted a neighbor. I didn't know what it meant, but I wasn't one to question the rules; I did as I was told. On April 20, 1945, the order came to hang out the Nazi flag in honor of Adolf Hitler's birthday. I was seven years old by then, but of course, I still didn't really grasp what was going on. All I knew was that we still had shortages of food and clothing, and all the men were still gone to war, except a few older ones who appeared on the streets now and then.

I did quite well in school despite the fact that I had little time to devote to my homework. I had so many chores: go to the store, go begging for food, or taking care of baby Guenter. Ilse or Traute helped, but it seemed like I was asked more often.

CHAPTER 3
WILHELMSHAVEN IN THE WAKE OF WAR

After some 84,000 bombs had been dropped in the area of Wilhelmshaven between 1939 and 1945, the war finally came to an end. One day, when I was seven years old, I heard the neighborhood kids calling me, "Gerda, Gerda, let's go see the tanks!" We ran as fast as we could to see the huge, rattling machines. In our imagination, we thought they were big monsters. Allied soldiers poked out of the opened tank hatches and tossed us candy, gum, and Knaeckebrot, a popular cracker-like bread. Scampering next to them, we followed the tanks all the way to Freilichgratstrasse, the nearby main street. We waved, screamed, and raised our arms for more goodies. With so many years of hardship and scarcity behind us, this small display of excess truly felt like a celebration. Even the people in the crowd— mostly women—seemed friendlier than usual. We children felt the excitement in the air and easily believed that now everything would be all right. Little did we know that the hard times would continue to follow us.

Since Ilse, Traute, and I were all school-age now, outsiders could scrutinize our lives more thoroughly. Soon, the teachers noticed our emotional and physical neglect. One day during the summer, as I sat by the window watching for Ilse to come home, I saw a lady with a briefcase approaching our building. I heard a loud knock at our door, so I ran to open it. Standing before me was a lady who was smartly dressed in business attire. She looked so professional, and I wondered what she wanted. She introduced herself as Frau Hildegard Rechler from Social Services and demanded to see my mother.

After my mother invited the lady in, they started talking. I was able to eavesdrop from the other room since the woman's booming voice easily penetrated the wall. Sternly, she told my mother, "You'd better start taking care of your children; otherwise, we'll have to put them in foster care." I felt sorry for my sick mother because she tried as best as she could to care for us. But then the harsh voice became gentle as she explained to my mother that we were eligible for welfare. This was music to my ears! I was too young to fully understand the concept of "welfare," but even I realized that we might get food stamps. What a relief that a grown-up was able to see the desperate nature of our existence, someone who knew that my mother was too depressed and overwhelmed with everything she had to bear. As I listened with intense interest, I also learned that the woman planned to send someone from the Red Cross to locate our father because we had no contact with him for a long time.

I felt sad when the woman left; she was the only adult in our lives who seemed able and willing to take care of us. I gazed at my mother. She looked so frail and disconnected, sitting there with her hands in her lap. But I was raised to be practical. I asked, "Will we get help now? Will we have enough food? Will we get new dresses?"

One day, not long after the woman's visit, Ilse, Traute, and I were lounging on our beds. Mother entered the bedroom, holding a piece of paper in her hand. She did not look happy. Taking a deep breath, she said, "I have bad news. Your father died in Russia, so he's not coming back." We were speechless for a moment but rather unaffected by his death. After all, we really didn't know him because he was gone too long. I noticed my mother didn't shed a tear either. I guess the war had made us numb. I certainly didn't feel the loss; I was happy that now we would get more money from the government. The next day, my mother went to the Rathaus City Hall to fill out the necessary paperwork.

In addition to welfare, we occasionally received care packages from America. Actually, I almost forgot about them until my brother Guenter recently reminded me. "Don't you remember how we enjoyed them?" he asked. "They saved our lives." The Red Cross also distributed clothing, shoes, and other items to needy families. I don't have a strong recollection of that part of my life, but I do remember the wooden clogs we got—a gift from Holland. They were stiff and noisy, but they kept our feet dry. How special that was!

I am thankful to the many countries that contributed food and goods to the war-stricken German people. We will always be grateful for those kind gifts.

⎯⎯⎯ ‿ₘₒₒₑₜₒₒₜₑₒₒₘ ⎯⎯⎯

By this time, more food was available, and the lines were shorter at the grocery store. Yet, each day, I still struggled to find enough food for all of us. It seemed like I carried the responsibility to beg, borrow, or steal food, but my siblings probably had to do some, too. I do remember my mother telling me, "*Du bist die Beste.*" You are the best!

A child should not be admired for being the best thief, and I often wondered how much of my difficult life was due to the circumstances of war or if it was just my stoic German upbringing. My siblings and I never felt an embrace, a nurturing touch, or a sign of tenderness, nor did we hear expressions of praise or love. Since it is impossible to erase the war from my childhood, I will never know.

The one distinct memory that is firmly lodged in my memory is that I always felt cold. Also, our shoes, handed down from one child to another, became so worn that there were no soles left. We tried to mend them with string, but that didn't last either. Our mother often kept us out of school because we were too hungry or had no shoes. No wonder we were so glad when spring arrived. Although northern Germany never got really hot in the summer, the snow, icy temperatures, and freezing cold rains were gone for a while.

There is one day of my childhood, at about age eight, that I wish I could erase. It started out fine. A bunch of girls, including my sister Traute and I, were walking home from school. During the ten-minute trek, we chatted among ourselves, not paying too much attention to our familiar surroundings. Suddenly a man approached me and asked, "Are you customers of Kohlen Otto?"

I knew we got our coal from that particular distributor, so I replied, "Yes."

He smiled at me and asked if I wanted to pick up the new membership card. Since I wanted to be helpful to my mother, I agreed. It would save my mother a trip, so I went along with him.

I felt uneasy when we walked past the entrance to Kohlen Otto, so I asked where we were going.

The man explained, "Oh, he has a table set up right behind the building."

I continued to follow him like any obedient child would. As we got close to a big pile of hay, he snatched me up and threw me on it. I screamed as loudly as I could. Then he stuffed a handkerchief in my mouth and threatened to throw my shoes in the brook if I did not stop yelling. He told me he wanted to see if I could have babies. When he raped me, I blacked out. After he finished brutalizing me, he let me go.

I stumbled home, sobbing all the way, with my shoes in my hands. When I entered the apartment, my mother was sitting on the couch reading something. She did not lift up her head to acknowledge me, nor did she notice my sobs. I figured she was looking over some type of government form; we never had a newspaper, a book, or a magazine in the house.

Devastated, I went to my room, flung myself on the bed, and cried until I had no more tears left. So, another unrecoverable part of my youth had been brutally stolen, and I could do nothing but bury the hurt deep inside me.

—————⁓⁓⁓⁓⁓⁓⁓⁓⁓—————

Every Saturday was bath time. Since there was little wood or coal for the stove and not enough fuel for the bathroom's heater, we took sponge baths. My sisters and I were assigned to bathe Guenter. This added chore diminished the time to complete my homework, but my complaint went unheeded.

In addition to being my teacher, Herr Harms was also the school's principal, and he was strict. One of my daily assignments was to write an essay; however, with so many chores to do, I often failed to write one. Sometimes, I left the house a little early in the morning and sat on the curb to finish my homework on the way to school.

Since my teacher was also strict, he ruled the classroom with his exacting standards. For instance, every Monday morning, he inspected our backpacks. If the contents were unorganized, he shamed and ridiculed the unfortunate student in front of the whole class.

Another example: If Herr Harms caught someone biting their nails, he rapped their fingers with a stick. I was not a nail-biter, so I never felt the pain. The punishment must have hurt a lot; the children cried, but Herr Harms continued to hit them.

43

He inspected under our fingernails to see whether they were clean. If one of the girls had dirty fingernails, she had to show them to the boys and vice versa. It was humiliating. Also, Herr Harms checked our shoes to see if they were clean and polished.

Oddly enough, despite his stringent manner, I liked my teacher. Herr Harms praised me for my intelligence, and his compliment made me feel good about myself.

Soon, my school offered a physical education class, but the nearest gym was a twenty-five-minute walk away. In the summer, our PE classes included swimming, but the pool was about thirty minutes away, so we didn't do either of these activities more than once a week or so. I did not go swimming because I didn't have a bathing suit. Although the teacher knew I couldn't participate, he made me walk to and from the pool. Silent and sad, I sat on the bench until the class was over, watching the other children have fun with their swimming lessons.

───── ·ᴡᴡᴏᴄᴇᴛᴏᴏᴛᴇᴏᴏᴡᴡ· ─────

After the war, it was hard to get basic hygiene items. There wasn't any soap to wash our clothes or take a bath. We didn't have toothbrushes or toothpaste, and I remember using my fingers to brush my teeth with salt. I'm not sure if everyone else had to do without these basic necessities, but I know my family didn't have them.

Coupled with a lack of supplies and my mother's inability to care for us, we often suffered from blisters and boils. Scratching at the itchy sores made them worse. Ilse, Traute, Guenter, and I all developed a bad case of scabies. Poor hygiene was probably the culprit, but it might have spread through the wounded soldiers returning from the war.

With all four of us children ravaged by scabies, we were grateful when Social Services once again intervened on our behalf. (Many years later, my sister Ilse, who still lives in Wilhelmshaven, told me that her teacher had asked the agency to pay us a visit.) A woman from Social Services came to our house and asked to see our mother.

"I heard that you're all sick. I will make sure you go to the doctor." My mother overheard the commotion and came out of the bedroom.

The woman addressed her. "Frau Hartwich, have you taken a good look at your children lately?"

"No, I'm not feeling well these days," she said.

The woman notified my mother, "Well, I'm going to make arrangements to have your kids picked up tomorrow and treated."

Just as the woman promised, a car arrived the next morning and took us to the hospital. Ilse was eleven, Traute was eight, I was seven, and Guenter was two. What a relief! For the next several days, we would be well-fed while getting rid of our itchy scabies. It's sad to think that we dreamed about plentiful food and abundant supplies when other children dream about castles and handsome princes and beautiful princesses. But our world—and our dreams—revolved around the practical concerns of day-to-day life.

Of course, the hospital trip was not as pleasant as I thought it would be. We were all going to stay in the same room, which made us feel safe. Then the nurse arrived and gave us instructions.

"Find a bathroom, remove your clothes, and hop into the bathtub.

Be sure that you stay down and soak your entire body," she directed.

It seems like I was in the tub for a long time. When the nurse came back with a big brush in her hand, I knew that it would hurt, and indeed, it did. After she scrubbed my body with its raw sores, she rolled me up in a huge white towel. I stayed wrapped up like that for a long time, and when the nurse returned, she yanked the towel off me. That hurt as much as the scrubbing did. I felt like crying, but I was too afraid.

I asked where my siblings were, and the nurse told me they were getting the same treatment next door. After she dressed me in a clean nightgown, the doctor came in and examined me. His diagnosis of an infectious skin disease was not surprising, and he administered some ointment to my oozing boils. Then he looked at the sores on my feet. "We'll have to open those up," he said. Picking up a pair of scissors, the doctor cut them all open. When he was finished, he remarked, "You're such a good girl. You didn't even cry."

Oddly enough, this was the first time I had been commended for not crying, despite the fact that I had been the same good little girl all my life.

As my siblings and I were all reunited in the same room, we shared our traumatic experiences. One good thing, however, was the promise of food. Each of us was thrilled to get a steaming bowl of split pea soup. It was so good! When the nurse asked who would like more, we quickly raised our hands. Instead, she returned with bowls of bread soaked in milk.

"I'm sorry we ran out of split pea soup," she apologized after looking at our disappointed faces, "but make sure you finish this."

As soon as she left the room, we all agreed that this stuff wasn't edible. So we tried to devise a method of disposing of the horrible soup. I looked around. The room had a washbasin but no toilet.

I suggested that maybe we could squeeze the bread through the sink drain. We considered this plan but decided we could not take a chance on clogging it up. Then I thought that if I sneaked down the hall and brought back some toilet paper, we could wrap up the bread and throw it out the window. It was not a bad idea until I looked at the tall window more carefully. I noticed that it tilted open only at the top to let in the fresh air. That plan wouldn't work either. We solved our problem by pouring the soup into Guenter's night potty. The nurse came in and turned off the lights, and that was the end of our first day.

The next morning, our mother came for a visit. She looked exceptionally well and even had a smile on her face. Perhaps not having the responsibility of caring for us eased her burden. I recall how eagerly she said, "You have it so good here, and you don't have to do anything."

We stayed in the hospital for about two weeks before returning home. The woman from Social Services promised to visit every two weeks to help our mother, and I was grateful that maybe her life would be better.

―――ᴠᴠᴠ∘ᴏᴏᴏᴏ∘ᴠᴠᴠ―――

After our hospital stay, we had to go back to school. I didn't mind the schoolwork; in fact, I loved learning about new things. But going to school meant I had to look at the other girls' pretty dresses. Mine were pretty old, and I wished I had a new dress once in a while.

Going back to school also meant I had to endure the harsh

cruelties of my teacher. If two students were caught talking, they would have to stand in front of the classroom. Then, the teacher would slap them both so hard in the face that it left red marks. When I was one of the unlucky offenders, I took my punishment without shedding a tear, no matter how great the pain and humiliation were. My teacher was not the only mean teacher; they all were "disciplinarians."

Our school did not have a library, nor did it have enough schoolbooks to pass out to each student. As soon as we were done with a class, the books had to be passed on to the next one. With such a scarcity of books, reading for pleasure was unheard of, so I missed the joy of escaping to an imaginary world.

Music class consisted of singing in a chorus; there simply was not enough money to acquire any instruments. During that hour, I pretended to sing. I blended into the throng of children by moving my lips. It didn't take me long to figure out that if I sat in the back, I could fake my way through the class while using that precious hour to do my homework.

Then I got caught. The teacher was so angry that he forced me to stand in front of the whole class and sing alone. I begged and pleaded for mercy, but he refused to retract the punishment. As I stood facing the crowd of children, my face turned red, and my heart pounded in my chest. I was so terrified that I could not squeeze out a single note.

I'll never forget the smirk on his face when he told me, "Gerda Hartwich, I'm going to have to fail you."

I thought this wouldn't have happened if I had enough time to do my work at home.

———— ᴠᴠᴠ·ᴏ·ᴏ·ᴇ·ᴛ·ᴏ·ᴏ·ᴛ·ᴇ·ᴏ·ᴏ·ᴠᴠᴠ ————

Nobody tore down the bomb shelter, so three years after

the war ended, the building stood as a reminder of those horrible years.

When the long summer days arrived, we noticed that some of the birds returned. What a pleasant surprise—it had been a long time since their songs serenaded us. For a moment or two, a sense of a normal future hung in the air. However, "normal" did not exist for my family, and our lives would change once more.

One night as we lay in bed, Ilse whispered, "Do you notice anything different about mama?"

"No," Traute and I said in unison.

Ilse raised her eyebrows. "Can't you see she's pregnant again?" "You know, you're right," Traute said. "She does look a bit heavier."

Of course, there was nothing we could do. Personally, I was not too happy about the situation.

I resigned myself to this new development. "Now we'll have even more work to do to care for a new baby," I said. "How did this happen? She's a widow, and there hasn't been a man around here for a long time."

We racked our brains, trying to guess who the father could be. We knew about her solitary bus trips into town; logically, she met someone there.

As it turned out, our mother was pregnant all right, but she didn't acknowledge her condition to any of us. Then, on October 29, 1948, the baby decided to make a grand entrance into the world. I ran a few blocks to fetch Dr. Kleber, and as soon as he arrived, we were sent away. Since it was raining, we couldn't go outside and play, so we huddled together in the basement. We were lucky that Brigitte Meyer, our next-door neighbor's daughter, was with us. Our ears were filled with Mother's agonizing screams from upstairs. Since Brigitte was older and wiser, she reassured us, "Don't be scared. The yelling doesn't last long—just while she's pushing the baby out."

Finally, Frau Meyer came down to announce the arrival of Wilhelm, our new baby brother. When we were allowed to come up, we noticed how pale and tired-looking our mother was as she held this new little person in her arms. Fortunately, mother and son were fine.

After our brother was born, we all had more chores to do. Now, I had even less playtime with my friends, and finishing my homework became impossible.

I was quick to figure out how to solve my homework problem. I knew Herr Harms assigned essays on a daily basis. The next day, he asked for volunteers to read theirs aloud to the class. If nobody volunteered, he would alphabetically summon the next student. I knew when "Hartwich" was going to be called next so that I would spend extra time on my assignment. Sure enough, one day, when nobody volunteered, he called on me. I was proud that I had fooled him. I received an excellent grade and knew I would be off the hook for a couple of weeks.

———————

December 15, 1948, is another day I'll always remember. There was a chill in the air while the autumn leaves gathered on the ground. Mother was still in bed recuperating from Wilhelm's birth.

I was ten years old and chatting with my classmate Helga Becker as we walked home that cool day. We were best friends, and she invited me to her house to do homework.

I really wanted to go, but I knew I had to ask my mother first. "Oh, why don't you just come?" she coaxed. "They won't miss you."

That sounded reasonable to me, so we skipped merrily all the way to her apartment. Her mother had been watching for us and came out as soon as we arrived. Frau Becker appeared uneasy. "Gerda, you have to go home. There's a surprise waiting for you."

A surprise was tantalizing, but I wasn't happy about going home right away: I would miss out on the snack Helga's mother had prepared. I was reluctant to go, but Frau Becker's serious attitude persuaded me to skedaddle without further delay.

I ran home as fast as I could, leaped up the entry steps two at a time and arrived at the apartment completely out of breath. A strange man was sitting in the living room. Who's that? I wondered.

"Gerda," my mother said with a monotone voice, "shake hands with your father." Obediently, I did. Then I shuffled to the couch, where I sat speechless and motionless across from him. Mother explained, "The Red Cross made a mistake. They lost his records, and he's been in a Russian prison all this time." While my mother spoke, I gazed at the stranger who professed to be my father. He was thirty-eight years old, but I thought he looked much older. His thin hair had receded, and his large nose was not becoming. From what I remember, his clothes were presentable. The most prominent feature was his cool, blue eyes. My thoughts drifted back to my mother's voice as she continued, "The Russians released him a week ago."

I was confused and not sure what to feel. In this German family—like so many others—emotions were not expressed. I noticed the beautiful nightgown he bought for our mother. Guenter got a toy, and each of us girls received a whole bar of chocolate. I wondered where he got the money to buy gifts.

After he was home for a day or two, he started to look for work, but so did a lot of others. He came home and felt dejected when he could not get a job.

"I guess it will take some time," he told our neighbor, Herr Meyer.

———∿∿∿᷈᷈᷈᷈᷈᷈᷈᷈᷈᷈᷈᷈᷈᷈᷈᷈᷈᷈᷈᷈᷈᷈———

When he telephoned his mother and sister, their joy at discovering he was still alive was overwhelming. They sent him a train fare to Hagen to visit them before he started working. While my father was gone, we were all happy. His presence in our home was still strange and awkward. When he returned, he was in good spirits. Among the things he brought home were lots of cookies, chocolates, and a live rabbit.

When it came time to slaughter the rabbit, he wanted us to watch as he prepared it for our meal. I was too young to know what to really expect. "I want to see it!" I wish I hadn't done that. The whole process was repulsive, especially when he slit the abdomen open, and the intestines came gushing out.

I will admit, though, that once the rabbit was in the pot and the delicious smell wafted in the air, I forgot all about the ugly part.

We enjoyed a great meal and went to bed with full stomachs and somewhat lighter hearts.

———∿∿∿᷈᷈᷈᷈᷈᷈᷈᷈᷈᷈᷈᷈᷈᷈᷈᷈᷈᷈᷈᷈᷈᷈———

The Christmas holiday in 1949 was the only one I remember from my early years. Our father had been home for more than a year by then, and our paternal grandmother from

Hagen decided to come for a visit. I hadn't seen her since I left Charlottenbrunn in 1942.

I wish I could remember what our grandmother looked like in those days. If she were like most German Omas, she would have worn a plain, dark dress, a practical hairdo, and a dour expression. No make-up, no hair dye, no-nonsense. When I look at photos of older women from this era, I notice how tightly folded their arms are over their chests, as if the existence of breasts were not something that a matronly woman should acknowledge.

The day of Oma's visit finally arrived. My father went to the train station to pick her up, and we all peered out the window, anxious for the first glimpse of their return. Mother was quiet, and I sensed her unease about the impending visit with her mother-in-law. We were so excited when we first spotted them coming around the corner. My father was carrying her bag, and I wondered what could be inside such a big suitcase. As they came up the stairs, I noticed how my father struggled with the heavy load.

Now, my curiosity was piqued. When the suitcase was finally opened, there were all kinds of goodies in there. She and Tante Erna must have baked for more than a week before that visit.

Most children look forward to sitting in their grandmother's lap and having a story read to them or hearing how much they have been missed and how big they've grown. But our family was not very emotional, so we didn't know how to react when we first saw our grandmother. Since there was virtually no contact between our family members over the years, it never occurred to us that she might have actually missed us.

When Christmas Eve day arrived, Ilse, Traute, and I

dutifully walked to church. During the forty-five-minute walk, our minds were focused on the Christmas celebration that awaited our return. I don't think the church service was meaningful to us since no one was a faithful Christian. We belonged to the church only because it was necessary to have a family member baptized, confirmed, married, or buried.

After the return trip from church that day, we ate a delicious dinner of bratwurst, mashed potatoes, and of course sauerkraut.

We all helped clean up the kitchen, and then we were ready for our celebration to begin. The Christmas tree was moved from one of the cold, drafty bedrooms into the living room. True to the real Christmas tradition, the adults decorated the tree while the children were at church. And the presents... there were so many, we could not believe our eyes! Tante Erna, who was quite a seamstress, had sewn three beautiful pleated skirts for us girls. Too bad she wasn't there so we could thank her. Our next presents were beautiful too. Oma knitted a sweater for each of us to match our new skirts.

Oma had a story to go with the sweaters. She knitted them during the time when the government needed to cut back on electricity. This happened two or three days a week.

We asked, "Oma, how could you knit in the dark?"

"Oh, you can count the stitches by feeling them," she laughed, "and I burned a lot of candles."

My sisters and I were overjoyed with these splendid clothes. How could we possibly thank her for making our Christmas so special? She sat on the couch with her hands folded and didn't say a word. We treasured those beautiful gifts, and the image of our grandmother sitting for hours knitting in the dark is unforgettable.

We opened a few small presents, like a Tuschkasten, a watercolor paint set. I had never seen anything like it. The final present was a whole bar of chocolate. I remember how I looked at mine for a long time and just smiled. Then we listened to some Christmas carols on the radio. I believe we played a game called *"Mensch aergere Dich nicht"* (Hey, don't get upset), which is the equivalent of "Aggravation" in the United States.

Now that I am older, I'm grateful to have shared some wonderful Christmases with my husband and children during the fifty years I've lived in America. Both children continue to follow some of these traditions with their own families. But that one Christmas day in Germany always stands out. In fact, I can't even remember any of the other Christmases while I lived overseas. Someday, I'd like to return to my homeland at Christmastime and maybe take a short river cruise along the Rhine. I want to experience the true spirit of Christmas—with Christ and God in my heart—to hear Christmas music sung in German and to visit the church where the Christmas story is retold. In recapturing these experiences, I feel that my soul may finally find absolute peace with everything that happened to me in my native country.

———ɹɯɹɔɔɔɹɔɔɹɔɔɔɹɯɹ———

I recall the time my father told Ilse and me to meet him downtown after school. He found a job collecting bricks, and we had to help him. As we walked the streets of Wilhelmshaven, we saw a lot of destroyed buildings, but there were also signs of rebuilding. Fortunately, there was no shortage of bricks to collect. Our father cleaned them with a chisel while Ilse and I carried and stacked them. At the end of the day, he counted them, and the total for the week determined his wages. Working for him after school meant that our homework suffered, but he never took that into consideration.

After a few days, our hands began to hurt from handling the rough, heavy bricks. He just shrugged. "Hold the bricks more loosely," he advised. After several weeks, I found a rag to cushion my hands so they would not hurt so badly.

It was backbreaking labor, and we were always tired and hungry. On weekends and during school vacations, we usually worked the whole day; after school, we worked for several hours. This job lasted for almost two years.

I do not have a picture of me working so hard. But I recently came across a newspaper photo in the Wilhelmshavener Zeitung, taken during those years, of a ten-year-old blond girl standing on a pile of rubble, doing exactly what I did. The only difference between her and me is that she sported a sausage roll on the top of her head, which was a popular female hairstyle of the day.

Printed with permission from WZ-Bilddienst.

My father worked at a variety of jobs, from wallpapering to welding. He preferred being a welder because it commanded a higher wage.

Father was a strict disciplinarian with a bad temper. It seems we always had to walk on eggshells around him because he got so angry over little things. If he were mad at my mother, he would give us kids a nasty stare-down. I can still feel his ice-cold blue eyes piercing through me.

One day, Mother went into town, and I was home with Guenter and Wilhelm. They were about six and two. When I heard my father screaming at my brothers, I rushed to the living room. My father hit Wilhelm so hard that the poor child's head struck the wall. Even though I was shocked by the display of violence, I went over to console my little brother. As I tried to hug away his tears, I noticed my father staring at us with those blazing, cold eyes.

After I told our mother what happened, I got "the treatment." Father called me a squealer and punished me by locking me in my bedroom. For a whole week, I was confined to that room after school. There was no heat and no books except my schoolbooks. I had food brought to me, but I was kept in isolation until Ilse and Traute came to sleep. I remember one day when I heard him in the hall and asked him to sharpen my pencil. He smiled and sharpened my pencil. This small act signified the end of my imprisonment. I was proud of myself because I was strong enough not to cry through the whole ordeal. This was one of the times I wished he had stayed in Russia or that the news of his death had been true.

—————

There was another incident with my father that I'll never forget. I was about fourteen years old and the proud owner of a bicycle. One early evening, I rode my bike to visit some friends. My curfew was nine o'clock, so I made sure I had plenty of time to get home. There would be hell to pay if I were late. As I pedaled quickly through the town, I heard a loud bang. I had blown out a tire! I knew that I shouldn't ride it any farther with a flat, so I walked the bike home. When I got to the corner before our house, I panicked: there was my father standing in the doorway with a belt in his hand.

As he whipped me, he said, "Don't you dare cry, or you'll get more of the same." I forced myself not to cry, and eventually, he stopped. Crawling up the stairs, I knew that no matter how sore my backside was, my heart ached even more. I glanced at my mother, who was too afraid to defend me, so she just turned away.

There were many such episodes of harsh punishment, both physically and verbally. We tried to obey his strict rules, but the beatings continued. As kids, we never understood why he glowered at us with such disapproval and hate swirling in his cold and unfeeling eyes.

CHAPTER 4
NO ROOM FOR GERDA

When I was attending school, the German academic system decided the future of each student's occupation. At the age of fourteen, every child was classified as either college material or destined to learn a trade.

Mr. Harms saw me as college potential. "You are a very bright girl. You should stay in school, so I'd like to see your parents." He handed me a note. "Make sure you give them this."

Glowing with the compliment, I skipped home like a little kid. I gave the teacher's note to my mother. She read it and then put it aside. "Let's wait until your father comes home," she said. I knew that wasn't a good sign. My mother continued, "Why don't you take the boys downstairs and play with them? I don't feel that well."

I mumbled under my breath about not having enough time to do my homework, but I did what I was told.

Later that evening, after sharing a meager supper, I showed my father the note from Mr. Harms requesting a parent-teacher meeting to decide my future.

"What's this nonsense?" he hissed. "You know we need everybody in this family to contribute to the household. I'll go and see your teacher tomorrow to let him know you won't be continuing school.

Then I'll find some work for you." He glared at me with those hateful eyes. "End of discussion!"

Nobody in our family worried when our father could no

longer find work in Wilhelmshaven. That meant he would have to leave the city to find a job, and his mean spirit would not be missed. He needed transportation for his search, but a car was too expensive, so he bought himself another motorcycle and traveled south. I often wonder if his pursuit of a paycheck was merely a ploy to desert his family. He promised to send part of his salary home, but we never saw a penny.

During my childhood, I didn't have much of a religious upbringing. I do know that I had been baptized as an infant in Bad Charlottenbrunn because we had family statistics where each new child was recorded. All family members were registered there, and it included information about their births, marriages, and deaths, as well as the births of their children.

But in Neuengroden, the Wilhelmshaven suburb where our apartment was, there was no church. The nearest Lutheran church was forty-five minutes away from our apartment, so we had confirmation classes at school. The pastor arrived there by bicycle once a week to teach us the basics of religion. The hour-long classes were not fun at all. None of the students respected this man. Often, we made fun of him behind his back.

A week before we were to be confirmed, the pastor gave us instructions on how to look smart in front of our parents. He said, "If you know the answer, raise your right hand. If not, raise your left."

It is ironic that one of the first lessons taught to us by a minister was how to be deceptive.

Finally, the Sunday of confirmation came. Eagerly, I waited for my father to come home because he was bringing me new shoes. When he finally arrived, I was so excited—I desperately wanted those black patent leather shoes. I held my breath as I opened the box. They were beautiful! I took them out, impatient to try them on, but when I eased my foot in one, it was too small. I was so disappointed I wanted to cry. My mother had a quick and practical solution. "Just curl your toes. They will have to do."

Then, I had to get ready for the ceremony. I opened the closet and pulled out the dress I got from the Red Cross. It was dark blue with a white collar. As it fell softly over my slender body, I realized it was the first nice dress I had ever owned. As the youngest girl, I usually got the hand-me-downs from Ilse and Traute. But not today—today, I felt like a princess.

At the church, we lined up in rows of two. As I glanced around me, I was quite pleased with how well I looked. Then we walked down the aisle to the front of the church, each of us carrying a small Bible. On top of the Bibles, we placed a small arrangement of flowers tucked into a white lace handkerchief. I remember the strong, sweet fragrance of lilies of the valley and white bellflowers when I buried my nose into them. The heady aroma was amazing, and I thought God had created these flowers just for this special occasion.

I was so caught up with the glamour of the ceremony that I didn't hear a word the pastor said.

Seasons came and went, and we all grew older. Ilse now had a job at the Olympia Company, a factory that made typewriters. She rode her bicycle every day to and from work—almost seven miles. Traute was helping a family with their children, and I was delivering bread for a local bakery. Guenter was now ten years old, and Wilhelm was five. My father still came home occasionally, and these visits were surprisingly peaceful. By now, we were used to living without him, but the extra money he brought home, although not very regular, was helpful.

Our mother became increasingly apathetic. The photo of her that follows was taken a few years before this time. Her color had never been rosy, but now anybody could see that she was not healthy.

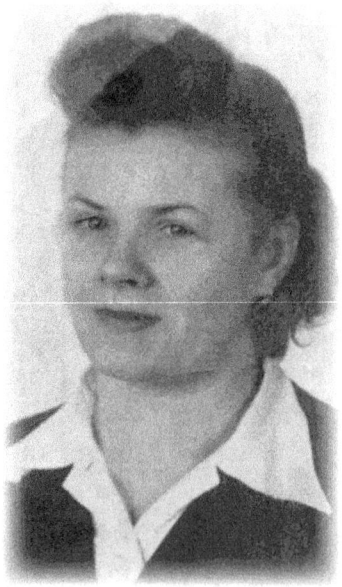

One day, she was sitting in the backyard when Frau Oldmann noticed her poor appearance.

"How are you doing?" she asked.

With a nod, Mother replied, "Fine."

Even Frau Oldmann knew that wasn't true. She must have mentioned her concerns to Dr. Kleber because soon after, he sent her mother a message to come see him right away.

The truth was that she had cancer. Perhaps she realized how sick she was when she saw the poster on the doctor's wall. "I read the seven warning signs of cancer, and I have them all."

The closest city with a hospital that had a radiation machine was in Goettingen. It was two and a half hours away by train.

When it came time for her to go for treatment, we helped her get dressed and pack a bag. A sense of hopelessness permeated her face as we hugged awkwardly and said goodbye. We watched and waved as she and my father turned the corner on their two-block walk to the bus that would take them to the train station. Before they slipped out of sight, my mother waved goodbye.

Even though Mother had been sick and dependent on us for many years, it was sad not to have her around. I was desolate, and I tried to find God somewhere in this heart-breaking situation. But I couldn't. Perhaps I should have learned how to pray in my confirmation class; unfortunately, I didn't.

I realized that we girls had to fight the sadness and despair by channeling our energy into caring for our brothers.

Father was fortunate to find a job in town, and we girls took care of the household. Now that Mother was away, he really ordered us around like soldiers. His critical and impatient manner became overbearing. Often, he would glare at us with that cold, disgusted expression if things didn't go his way. For instance, if he said, "Get me a screwdriver," and we didn't drop what we were doing right away, he would scream and call us lazy.

On the evenings he went out, we were glad he was gone. Since he was a heavy smoker, it was a relief to be able to breathe when he escaped on his motorcycle for a few hours. We often thought he might have a mistress somewhere, but that wasn't our main concern. Our priority was focusing on our mother.

We called the hospital once a week to inquire about our mother's progress, but the answer was always the same: "We don't know how long she has to stay. We will notify you."

We decided to send a package to the hospital to cheer her up. We bought cookies, chocolate, oranges, and a few other items, but Father found out how much we spent. He angrily reproached us, saying it wasn't necessary and we shouldn't have wasted our money. Incidents like this only encouraged us to hate the man a little more every day.

Three long weeks passed until we heard the good news: Mother was getting out of the hospital! We kept vigil by the window until a taxi pulled up in front of our house. She was pale and thin and did not look well at all, but we were happy to have our mother home again.

During the next few days, we concentrated on getting her healthy again. I remember making her a special drink—a glass of red wine with a beaten raw egg yolk in it. Her doctor had prescribed the concoction to help build up her red blood cells. Apparently, it worked; some days, she actually looked perky. One time, she and my father went to a movie, and she returned with a big smile on her face. She said the movie was a comedy and was good medicine for her soul. In fact, she was getting around so well that she started taking care of the boys again.

Sadly, that window of health closed up a couple of weeks later, and she was back in bed. The radiation treatments had not been successful. She started to lose a lot of weight and was becoming unsteady on her feet. We didn't have a telephone, but fortunately, Dr. Kleber lived a few minutes away. So I often sent messages to him, and he, in return, sent back medication with me or came to give our mother injections.

Ilse, Traute, and I took turns getting time off from work to stay with her, but it was difficult to watch her slip away. Dr. Kleber was honest when he said he couldn't guess how long she had to live. Her heart was strong, but the rest of her body was not. I feared her death was imminent when she looked in the mirror and asked, "Who is this woman?"

The days grew shorter and drearier as fall approached. The air was chilly, and it rained all the time. I moved to the room next to where she slept so I could be close to her. I no longer had to run to the doctor because he came every night to give her a shot of pain medication. By this time, she was totally bedridden.

One day, Frau Rechler, a lady from Social Services, showed up at our door. I suspect a neighbor must have called the agency since she had not visited us for a long time. Taking us aside, she asked about our plans after our mother passed away. I was stunned by the thought; nobody had mentioned anything about what we were supposed to do. Now confronted with the probability, Frau Rechler asked us to share our thoughts with her. Ilse, who was then nineteen, would continue to live in the rented room that was close to our apartment. Traute, seventeen, planned to live with an aunt in Nordheim, but I was uncertain about my future. The only thing I knew was that I was not going to spend one night alone with my father under the same roof.

As far as my brothers were concerned, Tante Erna agreed to take twelve-year-old Guenter, which left Wilhelm, who was only six years old. Who would take him? Our doubts were addressed quickly. Frau Rechler told us that our mother had made arrangements for him to be adopted, and Dr. Kleber already had a couple in mind. Although we were dumbfounded by this new development, we all agreed this was the best solution. I was amazed by my mother's prudence; she realized our father would not care for a child that wasn't his.

Fortunately, I was invited to live with my mother's oldest sister, Tante Gretel. I was elated that my wish would come true: I would not have to live alone with my father.

November 12, 1954, was a gray and rainy day. The air was cold, and our hearts were heavy. Mother had not eaten anything for a few days, and we all sat by her bed, waiting to see if she would take another breath. The doctor was still coming every day to give her shots for pain, so she was as comfortable as possible.

When she started making strange noises, it frightened us girls even more. It was decided that I should fetch Tante Hannchen, my mother's youngest sister, who lived about five miles away. It was almost midnight when I started on my bicycle, and the trip was difficult with only a small light to guide me. I made it safely to my aunt's house, knocked on the door, and woke up the family. She agreed to come and got dressed quickly, knowing her sister's death was near. I stayed with her two boys, Juergen, six, and Peter, an infant, so that she could ride the bike back to my house.

Exhausted from stress and the midnight physical workout, I soon fell asleep on the couch. A few hours later, Tante Hannchen returned. My mother had died.

Tante Erna came from Hagen for the funeral. Also, another sister from Nordheim arrived two days later. Our small church in Wilhelmshaven had a little chapel where my mother's viewing took place. This was the first time I had seen a dead person, but as I gazed at her face, she looked so peaceful. She had struggled so hard for so long; now, she was at rest. I don't know why I couldn't cry, but I didn't.

I don't remember how many people were present or what the minister said, except that he talked about life and death and reminded us that our dear Mother was with God. I had heard this message before, but I really didn't believe it. As we all walked behind her casket, I felt like I wasn't even present. After the service, the chauffeur from the funeral home drove us to the cemetery, where my mother would lie for eternity.

Her grave was mounded with flowers and wreaths. How ironic that she had never seen that many beautiful flowers in her life. I'm sure she would have preferred to enjoy them while still alive.

It's interesting to note that even today, Germans have a strong penchant for bringing flowers to almost every social occasion, whether a dinner party or a simple Kaffeeklatsch, a gathering of friends to share a cup of coffee and hear the latest gossip. Perhaps this fondness for flowers stems from the war: funerals were our only opportunity to see them.

Immediately after the funeral service, a small lunch was offered at the nearby Beerhalle, an informal restaurant. Those who joined us talked little about my mother; their focus was making final plans to take care of us children. In a daze, my siblings and I said our final goodbyes, not knowing when we would see each other again.

Tante Gretel and I took the train to Bentheim. We hardly spoke to each other during the long trip, and the screeching of metal against metal as the steam engine chugged along interrupted my thoughts. I was sixteen, and I was depressed.

I was reminded of my mother's death every time I glanced at the black armband I wore around the sleeve of my gray coat. In my culture, it was customary to wear black clothing for at least six months following the death of a family member. Since my wardrobe was limited, I wore only the black armband.

By the time the train arrived at my new home, I was too numb to feel anything.

My life in Bentheim proved to be uneventful. Each day passed like the one before, and I was terribly lonely. People were nice to me, but I missed my siblings. Besides, I was more accustomed to a larger city. Wilhelmshaven, a city with a population of almost 100,000, was more dynamic than Bentheim, which had only 6,000 people.

Since my aunt and uncle had two sons, there was no room for me in their small house. I was passed on to a family who owned a fish and vegetable store, and I worked in their store in return for room and board. I really couldn't complain; I had survived through worse conditions. In addition to my own room, I had three square meals a day.

The people I lived with were tolerable. On weekends, I visited my aunt and uncle and their two sons. When I visited, we often played games, and sometimes, the boys and I would go to a movie. I tried to keep myself occupied as much as possible, but my sadness didn't budge.

Although I wasn't expecting a lot of mail, I wished my family would write some letters to me. The isolation certainly intensified my despair, and I continued living like that for several months.

One evening, while having dinner with my host family, I sensed something was wrong. Then I was told a letter had arrived from my father, who requested my presence back in Wilhelmshaven. I was stunned because I hadn't heard a word from him since I left. I was glad that I would be reunited with my sisters—I missed them so. I can't say the same about my father.

I was also excited to go back to the city where I grew up. I packed my suitcase as fast as I could, and two days later, I was on the train, traveling back to Wilhelmshaven. As the train rattled back home, I wondered if my father had also sent for Traute.

I should have prepared myself for disappointment. There would not be room for Traute and me after all. My father had forgotten to mention that he had remarried—and that his new wife Dora had three children who lived with them. Once again, his thoughtless irresponsibility had disappointed me. Early in our relationship, I recognized how hard and unfeeling he was, but this last incident hit a new low.

When I realized that even my aunt Hannchen didn't have room for me, I was fortunate to find an elderly lady in town who had a nice, clean, comfortable room to rent. I earned a living at the Olympia Company, the same place that employed Ilse. A bicycle transported me to and from work, and on weekends, I would meet Ilse or Traute or spend a day with my aunt.

The city was coming back to life; many of the destroyed homes and businesses were being cleaned or rebuilt. Most of the bomb shelters were demolished or converted into apartments. The shelter near our school had been torn down, but in Shortens, a suburb on the outskirts of town where my sister Ilse and her family still live, the shelter remains. It can't be removed because it is surrounded by homes. The Americans once tried to dynamite it by first filling it with water, but that didn't work. The old relic is an ugly reminder of the war, but it has been put to good use in recent years: a mountain-climbing organization trains there.

At work, I managed to have a good time, even though most of my co-workers were married and had little in common with a young, single woman. Sometimes, I met my sisters at dance classes so we could show off our new steps at the dance hall on Saturdays. We also spent time at the movies and going to local fairs. Once in a while, we went on a picnic and enjoyed the sunshine and fresh air. Like the city itself, we were coming back to life. But I still missed my brothers Guenter and Wilhelm. The family wasn't complete without them.

One day our father asked to see us. He told us that he had written to our Tante Erna in Hagen and found out that Guenter, now fifteen years old, was feeling lonely. My father thought it would be best if Guenter returned to Wilhelmshaven to live with him and his wife. Guenter could attend classes with his friends and would be near us as well.

Two weeks later, Ilse, Traute, and I went to pick up our brother at the train station. There he stood, two feet taller than we remembered, his wavy hair combed back, and his blue eyes filled with tears. This was one time our stoic nature crumbled away, and my sisters and I zealously hugged him. We took the bus back to my father's apartment, and he and Dora seemed pleased to have him back.

Now I wondered about Wilhelm. Where was he? Was he happy? Was he with a good family? My father didn't know and really didn't seem to care.

It was 1956. I was 18 years old, and Wilhelmshaven had been reborn from the ashes. New buildings mushroomed, and old apartment houses boasted bright coats of paint. Lush trees and bushes offered a pleasing palette of colors, and people walked in the park. It seemed peaceful. The stores displayed a bounty of goods we had not seen before. There were dresses, linens, shoes—it was absolutely amazing. When the stores were closed, the exciting thing to do was to go to the movies, then stroll up and down Main Street, and maybe stop for cake and coffee at a café.

I dated some young men and experienced a kiss or two but had no plans to get involved with anybody, at least not yet. But as I got older, I dreamed about having a nice family. I asked God to send me a handsome, kind, and considerate husband with parents who I could be proud of. Then, I got a little more specific. "I don't want to be too greedy, God," I ventured, "but would you make sure my husband earns enough money to support a family so I don't have to pinch every penny?" Little did I know my wish would come true, but that was far into the future.

———

I wasn't feeling well for several days. My tired body could not get rid of the pain in my stomach, so I decided to make an appointment with our old family doctor, Dr. Kleber.

The day I went to visit him, the wind was blowing so fiercely that I had to use all my energy to pedal my bicycle. The difficult trip was worth it when Dr. Kleber welcomed me with his genuine concern for me.

The good doctor was tall with a strong chin. His thick, dark hair framed a pair of soft, brown eyes. "What's wrong with you, dear child?" he asked. After examining and questioning me, he figured out my problem. "I have a suspicion that you may have an ulcer. First, I'd like for you to go to a specialist, and then I'll be able to treat you. Don't worry, you'll be fine."

His kind words were soothing, and I was amazed by the amount of time he spent with me. But then he caught me completely off guard when he asked, "Would you like to know more about Wilhelm?"

Tears sprang to my eyes. "Yes!" I had missed my little brother very much.

Back in those times, the confidentiality issues about adoptions were nonexistent, so Dr. Kleber told me all about the husband and wife who were in their mid-forties when they adopted Wilhelm. He also was able to tell me where Wilhelm's adoptive parents lived. Then, the doctor asked me a question that took me by surprise. He asked if I would like to live there too. Is it possible that I might finally be a part of a real family? Without hesitation, I said yes. I was so excited that my ulcer seemed to have disappeared. That night, I had a difficult time falling asleep.

Almost two weeks later, I was admitted to the hospital for treatment of a stomach ulcer. One of the things I had to do was drink milk, and I still hated it with a passion. The doctor warned me about not drinking my milk. "You'll never get well," he said. Another phase of my daily treatment required me to swallow medicine that tasted like kerosene. After I drank the liquid, I had to lie down and rest on each side for ten minutes. The regimen made me almost sicker than the ulcers did.

I was in there for almost six weeks, and I missed my family terribly. Not one of my siblings visited, even though there was public transportation available. I never expected my father to visit; he was too wrapped up with his new family. In retrospect, I believe my sisters' lack of compassion stemmed from the ordeal of surviving the war. A lack of goodness and kindness in our lives had crushed our ability to show love and affection.

It's like we were each emotionally adrift in our own little boat.

———ᴠᴠⁱ⁰ᵍᵉᵗᵒᵍᵗᵉᵒᵒᴠᴠⁱ———

As I suffered through those treatments day after day, I held on to the comforting thought that if my mother were alive, she would have come to see me. After all, she had visited me in the hospital years ago after I had a bicycle accident.

After I was discharged from the hospital, I toyed with Dr. Kleber's suggestion about living with Wilhelm and his adoptive parents. As soon as I was physically able, I rode my bike to his office, and the doctor reassured me that Wilhelm's guardians were still expecting me.

Once again, I packed my suitcases, said goodbye to my aunt and her family, and reassured them that after I settled in, I would come back for a visit. My aunt and uncle took me to the bus station so I could make the fifteen-mile trip to the other side of Wilhelmshaven.

During the long bus trip, my nerves started to fray. Once again, my thoughts churned in my head: Would I be accepted into the family? How would they treat me? I was so preoccupied with my dilemma that it took me a while to notice an elderly lady standing in the aisle. As I focused on her face, I realized how sad she looked. Where are my manners? I thought she was old and probably uncomfortable. Her face lit up when I offered her my seat, and she thanked me profusely.

However, my apprehension about this new chapter of my life returned. Tears prickled the back of my eyes, but I was an expert at holding them back.

Finally, I arrived at my destination. I took a cab from the bus stop, the last leg of my journey, and eagerly awaited the reunion between my little brother and me. As I stood in front of the three-story house, I mustered up the courage to ring the doorbell. I hope they are just as excited as I am, I prayed fervently. When Frau and Herr Becker opened the door, they both shook my hand. I next saw Wilhelm, and he was told to greet me. Politely, he came forward and extended his small hand.

I was disappointed with the indifferent formal greeting. I had imagined big hugs and lots of chatter about missing each other through the years. The invitation to come inside smoothed over the awkward moment.

They requested that I should address them as Herr and Frau Becker. This was not an unusual demand since Germans are rather formal people. But I was shocked when they made it clear that Wilhelm should call me Fraulein Gerda. As "Miss" Gerda, I would not be recognized as his sister. I was heartbroken, but once again, I refused to show my emotions.

Their apartment turned out to be nice. The living room was rather large, with a comfortable couch and a cocktail table that could be adjusted higher for meals. The China closet displayed some lovely things: pretty vases, nice dishes, and some crystal pieces. They showed me their master bedroom, the bathroom, and a cozy room for Wilhelm. The kitchen was small but functional. As the tour came to an end, I realized there was no room specifically for me. Mrs. Becker pointed to the couch and said I would have to sleep there. I hope the disappointment didn't show too much on my face. Being practical, I resolved myself to the situation and was grateful to be here.

Frau Becker cooked us a simple meal, although I don't remember what I ate. At that moment, I didn't care about food or lively conversation; I only had eyes for my newfound little brother. His face had become rounder, and his beautiful blue eyes reminded me of our mother.

After dinner, I unpacked my suitcases. There was a small

dresser to keep my neatly folded clothes, and I hung my dresses in the hall closet. Frau Becker gave me a set of sheets and a pillow so I could make up my bed. Then everybody said goodnight, and again, Wilhelm was instructed to shake my hand.

That was the end of my first day with the Beckers, but I was too anxious to fall asleep right away. My thoughts kept wandering back to Wilhelm, my mother, and my siblings. I finally gave in to quiet tears. Did I do the right thing by coming here? At last, I drifted off to sleep. For the moment, I would be near my little brother.

The alarm clock shook me out of a deep slumber, and my limbs were heavy as I rose to greet the day. I had some tea and bread for breakfast. Frau Becker packed me lunch, and I went to work at the Olympia factory.

Over the next several days, the Beckers gave me clear signals about revealing my blood ties to Wilhelm: nobody should know. I was forbidden to be alone with my brother in case someone might recognize us as siblings. The forced separation was wearing me down, but I couldn't see a way out. What broke my heart the most was that my little brother and I could only hold hands under the table, which we did whenever we got the chance.

The strained relationship grew. Herr Becker made me uncomfortable with his odd stares, and I began mistrusting him. Somehow, I knew this wasn't the place for me after all. Once again, I found myself unloved and unwanted. Why couldn't I find my place in the world? I was too young to figure out what to do next. I would have prayed to God for answers if I could have been convinced there was a God, but even He seemed unavailable.

I didn't have to wait long for my fate to be decided for me.

One day after work, Frau Becker wanted to talk to me. With a serious look in her eye, she mentioned her cousin, who owned a sweater factory in Kiel. Kiel was a few hundred kilometers away, close to the Baltic Sea. "Would you be interested in moving there?" she offered in a cool voice. "They have a daughter, Christa, who's about your age, and a son, Peter, who's two years younger. You might be happier with them." She looked at me with unblinking eyes. I had the feeling she was no more pleased with me than I was with her.

Here was my situation: I couldn't acknowledge my little brother, nor was I comfortable with the couple that adopted him. I reasoned, what was I doing here? Wilhelmshaven was where I grew up, but it harbored many bad memories. My family ties certainly weren't binding me here; my siblings were independent and lived their own lives. My father was remarried and busy with his new brood. We seldom saw each other.

The only other consideration was a young man named Horst, a mechanical engineer I met where I worked. Although there was a definite attraction between us, I surmised that his upper-class social status would prevent the relationship from going anywhere. I remember that he drove a white Volkswagen. For a long time afterward, whenever I saw one, my heart jumped.

I made my decision to go to Kiel. Now I had to tell the Beckers, which wasn't difficult at all. But telling Wilhelm I was leaving was another story. The look in his eyes was heart-wrenching before he ran from the room.

Frau Becker contacted her relatives and told them when to expect me. I let Ilse and Traute know I was moving, but I didn't get much resistance from them. I also notified my father about my impending move, but my departure didn't faze him. The only one who would miss me was Wilhelm, and I rationalized that he would be all right. Although his adoptive parents didn't lavish affection on him, at least he had food, clothing, and shelter.

The day came for my departure, and my few belongings returned to my suitcase. Politely, we all shook hands goodbye. Wilhelm and I made little eye contact; otherwise, we both might have cried.

Ilse offered to see me off at the train station, and I was delighted that my departure wouldn't be so lonely after all. While waiting for the train, Ilse and I were a little awkward around each other. We really didn't know what to say to each other. I think we both felt relieved when the loudspeakers announced my train's departure. Our embrace was a little stiff, but we talked about visiting each other.

"Please, let's stay in contact," I said.

As the train picked up speed, I watched Ilse waving her white handkerchief until I could see it no more.

I was almost twenty and still desperate for a loving, functional family. I listened to the sound of the massive iron engine taking me farther away from those meager roots that were all I had ever known. The sun was shining brightly, but it couldn't dispel the gloom in my heart. I resigned myself to my unknown future, but I held a glimmer of hope that my next move would give me peace.

———

When I arrived in Kiel, I pulled out a white handkerchief from my pocket and held it in my right hand. This was the prearranged signal to find my new boss's sister, who would carry a red carnation in her left hand. We found each other near the restaurant. Among the noisy sounds of the train station, we introduced each other. Her name was Irene. She didn't drive a car, so we took a streetcar to the suburban town of Kiel-Garden. This was where the Scheff family, owners of the sweater factory, lived.

As soon as Irene and I arrived, the whole family had gathered around to welcome me, and they all seemed pleasant. Everyone was chattering around me in the entryway, but I scarcely heard a thing. Looking past the small crowd of people, I was overwhelmed by the luxurious décor of their living room. Exquisite Persian rugs adorned the well-maintained wooden floors. The drapes were beautifully tailored and framed the windows with a regal flair. Mentally, I convinced myself I could get used to these lavish surroundings.

Then, I was introduced to Frau Schliebener, the housekeeper. She was a short and stocky woman of mature years. As we shook hands and looked into each other's eyes, there was an emotional connection. Her warm welcome conveyed her sense of kindness. Frau Scheff, the owner of the business, invited us all to have supper in the dining room. This area was also spacious and expensively furnished with a carved mahogany table and chairs. The matching China closet was simply huge and housed an abundance of bone China and several art objects. I noticed how the table was carefully set.

At first, the conversation focused on what my duties entailed and my room and board. I was delighted to learn that I would eat all my meals with the family, especially since Christa and Peter would be there. I enjoyed listening to them as they laughed and teased one another. Sadly, I realized my siblings and I never shared that easy banter.

The second floor of the Scheff's home was like a separate apartment, and my bedroom was the smallest of its rooms.

Christa occupied the big living room with a sleeper bed, and Peter was in the next room. As I remember, neither Peter nor I had heat in our rooms; only Christa had that luxury.

My room had a slanted ceiling, which made it feel even smaller. It contained a Kleiderschrank, a clothes cabinet, a little table, a chair, and a lamp. The bed was pushed up against the wall, and if I wanted to look out of the window, I had to stand up because it was high. I unpacked my few things and took my toiletries to the bathroom. Then, I discovered the apartment had no hot water while brushing my teeth and washing my face. Apparently, the only place to take a warm shower was downstairs. I would have to get used to the cold water in the mornings and at night. My one small extravagance was my cozy featherbed, and soon I fell asleep.

The next morning, I was treated to a huge breakfast, an unheard-of pleasure. Armed with a full stomach, I was ready to be introduced to the employees of the sweater factory. Everyone was gracious as they smiled and welcomed me.

The Scheff's company had twenty-five employees, and during the holidays, everyone had to work hard to fill the large orders. First, I had to learn how to operate the complicated machines. Once I mastered them, I often worked evenings and weekends. When I wasn't working, I was training new employees. For the first time in my life, I earned decent wages enough to buy myself some nice clothes. Up until this point, I never would have considered the prospect that life could actually be fun. The only misgiving I had concerned my fellow workers. Since I lived with the boss, the employees were cautious about including me in their gossip.

One bright spot in my daily life was befriending Frau Schliebener. When I had the time, I helped her with the housework just by being near her. As we grew closer, we exchanged the tragedies of our lives, including the loss of her husband and two sons in the war.

Sometimes, I stopped by to visit her before going to my room. She had a record player, and I enjoyed sitting and listening to the music with her. One song in particular had sad lyrics:

Hast du dort oben vergessen auf mich?

Es sehnt doch mein Herz auch nach Liebe sich.

It translates as "Have you forgotten me, up above? My heart, too, longs for love." Frau Schliebener played this song often because she missed her loved ones. But she never complained. When I worked on weekends, she and I shared coffee and cake in the afternoon.

───✧◦✧◦✧◦✧───

I also met Inge, who worked in the bookkeeping department and was closer to my age than Frau Schliebener. We became good friends and enjoyed more activities together. For a fun night out in town, we went to the movies. Inge and I loved to dance, and there was one particular young man I admired while on the dance floor.

His name was Dieter, and his family was wealthy and educated. His father was the president of the Kiel shipyard, with 11,000 people working for him. One time, Dieter invited me to his home, and he and his mother entertained me with a piano duet. The rich notes floated in the air and filled my heart with joy. Then, a dark cloud hovered over me when I realized I would never be accepted into this family.

I still carried within me a deep sense of unworthiness, as if I didn't quite belong anywhere. I broke off an upcoming date with Dieter, determined to pre-empt the inevitable rejection.

Oddly, my life spiraled downward after I rejected Dieter's interest. I began to feel overworked at the factory and outclassed in the Scheff's home. Christa started treating me like a servant.

She made her position clear: I'm the daughter, you're the employee.

My dream of belonging to a real family receded farther away. I felt abandoned and lonely once again.

There was one other thing that weighed heavily on my mind. There were a few days when I didn't feel well, and since my mother died of cancer, I feared I would succumb to the same dreaded disease. At least I could do something in this situation, so I made an appointment to see a doctor.

On the day of my appointment, as I was ready to leave the house, Frau Scheff couldn't resist offering her opinion. "The doctor isn't going to find anything wrong," she predicted. "He'll put a flashlight up your rear end, and that will be it." I was shocked and disgusted by her crude remark. I didn't think an upper-class person would say such a thing, and on that day, I lost some respect for my boss.

What a relief when the diagnosis came in: I didn't have cancer; I had a disease that is referred to today as irritable bowel syndrome. The doctor predicted I would feel better in a few days with proper diet and medication.

The year was 1958, and my twentieth birthday was fast approaching: October 7. I thought that perhaps the Scheff family would acknowledge my special day. Flowers would have been nice. By the time lunch arrived, nobody from the entire factory had wished me a happy birthday. I could not contain my disappointment anymore, so I blurted out,

"Today's my birthday!"

Everyone in the lunchroom turned their heads and gazed at me. Frau Scheff interrupted her conversation with someone else, pointed to the shop, and said, "Why don't you pick out a sweater from the shop?"

While the thought was generous, and I appreciated the gift, I would have preferred someone to take note of my special day. Nobody from my family in Wilhelmshaven sent me a card. When lunch was over, I went back to work with a heavy heart.

I needed to take a vacation to perk up my spirits. I decided to visit my aunt and grandmother in Hagen. I had traveled by train many times before, but not recently. I was also nervous about transferring to Hamburg, one of the largest cities in Germany. Taking a taxi to the train station was the easy first leg of my trip, although I probably overtipped the driver. Inside the noisy, bustling station, I asked a conductor to point out the train going to Hamburg. I checked and rechecked the signs on the cars to make sure I boarded the right one. After I found my seat, I heaved a sigh of relief and tried to relax.

As the train rumbled away from the platform, the whistle blew its shrill sound. I gazed out the window, watching the scenery zip by. Children waved. I waved back. I noticed people doing ordinary things, like weeding their gardens and picking fruit. Soon, the pastoral scene out of my window changed as the city of Hamburg came into view.

Once again, I was seized with fright. I had to convince myself that I could handle it. Gerda, I mentally reasoned, as long as you have money in your wallet and speak the language, you can't get lost!

With renewed courage, I disembarked from one train and managed to get on the right train to Hagen. By now, I was starving; I'd forgotten to eat. Luckily, a beverage cart came around, and I ordered a soda and a hot dog. A few hours later, I arrived at my destination.

The instant I got off the train, I started searching for my aunt and grandmother. I didn't see either one, and the panic returned. As a child, I had the same feeling once when I got separated from my mother. I chided myself again. You're not a little kid anymore. I did the prudent thing and called a taxi.

When I arrived at my grandmother's, she gave me a big, welcoming hug. After our initial greeting, we became concerned about Tante Erna, who had gone to the station to meet me. In a few minutes, she returned home. That's when we decided to play a trick on her. I hid behind the door and listened. "I couldn't find Gerda anywhere," she lamented. "I hope she's all right." She sounded upset; I couldn't let her anguish continue. "Here I am," I said as I stepped out from behind the door and hugged her. What a good sport; she wasn't mad, just happy to see me.

After a quick tour of their beautifully furnished apartment, we settled in for a long chat. The subject of their newfound religion came up, and I listened with fascination about their relationship with Jesus and how happy it made them. They mentioned their routine of reading the Bible twice a day and their fondness for gospel music. I thought they were being a bit fanatical. Since my faith was shaky at best, I felt uncomfortable. I discreetly brought my knitting to the table, and while they prayed, my needles clicked away quietly under the table.

These two wonderful women were good to me. They suggested I could live with them if I wanted. Unwilling to hurt their feelings, I told them I'd think about it. As our visit came to a close, I thanked them with all my heart, but I knew I'd never move there.

I returned to Kiel, worked hard, and saved some money. My budget allowed an occasional outing to the movies with my girlfriends, and I even went to the opera once.

I was invited by Hans, a nice young man I had met. I didn't want to admit that I never heard an opera before, but I was eager for the experience. The evening proved to be wonderful, like a dream I didn't want to end. Hans was a true gentleman—soft-spoken, polite, and respectful. He also treated me like a lady, a trait I admired and sought after when choosing a date. Of course, I was careful not to allow any of my dates the opportunity to take advantage of me.

Hans and I spent a lot of time together, going to the movies, dancing, and getting to know each other. He was curious about my background, so I divulged the basics of my family: I told him about my siblings, my mother's death, and my father's remarriage to a woman with three children. If the conversation leaned toward more personal events, I quickly changed the topic. I was too ashamed of my dysfunctional family to risk Hans's judgment; instead, I steered the conversation toward his family.

His father managed a telephone company, so Hans and his family lived in a well-to-do area. When he invited me to his home, I told him I was not ready to meet his parents. Just as I had done with Horst, I cut the relationship short, certain I'd be rejected. I was determined not to be hurt, so I stopped seeing him before my prediction could come true.

At night, as I lay in bed, I often wondered about my future. I asked God if He might send me a kind husband who earned a nice living. A small house would be nice, and some children. I wanted a family; I wanted to belong somewhere. I felt so alone in the world, and I was hoping that marriage might bring with it a family that would accept me just as I was. On countless nights, these thoughts lingered in my brain until I dropped off to sleep.

In the morning, the penetrating sound of the alarm clock always brought me back to reality. The truth of my life was a stark reminder that I was still the same lonely girl I'd been the night before.

I'd start each day by splashing my face with cold water before I trudged off to work. The feeling of being an outsider in the Scheff family intensified, and my designs for bettering my situation began to take a new tack.

Could I go to night school? I asked myself. I made a few inquiries by telephone, but what I found out was hardly encouraging. Classes were not offered in the evenings, and there was no government funding for people like me. My misfortune was compounded not only by war, poverty, and family dysfunction but also by a lack of educational opportunity.

CHAPTER 5
THE VISIT THAT CHANGED MY LIFE

One day, in the summer of 1960, I remember Christa Scheff handing me a letter. I recognized Tanta Erna's handwriting, and I quickly tore open the envelope. What a delight to learn that my cousin Rose and her six-year-old son Roy were coming from the United States to Hagen for a visit in two weeks. Tanta Erna wanted to know if I would like to come and meet them.

Rose and her husband Hjalmar, a native Norwegian, had immigrated to the United States in 1951. First, they settled in Brooklyn, New York, and later built a home in Griggstown, New Jersey.

Christa sensed my excitement and pleaded to let her in on my good news. I announced that I was going to meet my long-lost cousin. Running out of the room, Christa found her mother and told her my plans. A little later, Frau Scheff remarked, "I know you'll put in extra hours to get ahead on your work."

So I wrote back immediately, telling Tante Erna that I would love to come and meet Rose and her little boy. Two weeks later I was on the train again, and this time, the journey wasn't frightening at all. Maybe I was too preoccupied with reading a book about America I had bought before the trip. As the miles sped by, I learned that the country's population was diverse, a "melting pot" of people who came from every continent of the world. I tried to find a picture of the streets paved in gold, but there weren't any.

With a loud screech, the train ground to a halt at the

platform in Hagen. My aunt and I did not make arrangements to meet each other at the train station, so I looked for a taxi. To my surprise, I saw Tante Erna, Rose, and Roy anxiously waiting to pick me up. Rose, a tall young woman, had a friendly, gentle-looking face. As she wrapped her slender form around mine, she whispered in my ear, "I'm so glad we're finally meeting." I don't remember hearing those kind words, which were music to my ears.

Roy didn't speak German, but after a few days, we were able to communicate with hand gestures. We occupied our time together playing ball and board games. The close family atmosphere was so enjoyable to me.

One thing nagged me: Could I muster up enough courage to ask Rose about coming to visit her family in America? Perhaps God could be my ally. After all, my aunt and grandmother were very comfortable with their belief that God and Jesus were our saviors. If He were on my side, maybe my dream would come true. I didn't have to wait long to know my prayers were answered.

Shortly after breakfast the next day, I took a deep breath and asked Rose, "Could I come and visit you?"

She did not hesitate for a moment. "Of course you can; we'd love to have you!"

Now that I knew I was going to America, I toyed with another daring thought: I could make the visit permanent if I chose to immigrate. Rose and I discussed this new possibility. First, she said, I would have to get a sponsor to vouch for my character, to affirm I could support myself so I would not become a burden to the U.S. government. Being a sponsor was a big undertaking. If the immigrant could not find work, the sponsor would be liable for support. "I'll always find work," I reassured her. I also promised to return to my homeland if things didn't work out.

This was my golden opportunity to leave behind the bad memories of the war, and I could escape from my tyrannical father once and for all. I was ecstatic when Rose declared Hjalmar, and she would be honored to sponsor me. Silently, I thanked God for His help.

Rose's final week in Hagen seemed to fly by; soon, it was time for us to say goodbye. I felt such a kinship with this woman—my words flowed from my heart to my mouth: "Rose," I said, "thank you for trusting me and allowing me to come to America. I will work hard to support myself, and I promise not to be a burden to you or Hjalmar!" As tears of gratitude slid down my face, I happened to glance at Tante Erna.

"I guess I'm losing you too," she said wistfully.

Now that my future was established, I wanted to return to Kiel- Garden immediately so I could tell Frau Scheff about my intentions to immigrate to America. When I arrived home, however, there was a mountain of work to catch up with, so I put in extra evening and weekend hours.

The time came when I had to apply for my U.S. immigration application. I asked Frau Scheff for time off to visit the American Embassy in Hamburg, but she scoffed at my plan. I didn't expect a positive reaction, but her ridicule made me more determined.

At the embassy, I inquired about the possibility of immigrating to the United States. Within a week, I received an enormous application packet that contained about 300 questions. I was surprised when I came across this one: Are you planning to become a prostitute? At first, I was a little offended, but I understood the reason for the question.

It took several months for the U.S. Citizenship and Immigration Services to verify all my previous addresses. Then a letter arrived: I should report to Hamburg for a verbal interview and a medical checkup. Always skeptical, Frau Scheff didn't believe I would follow through on this venture. When I asked for the day off to go to Hamburg for my checkup, she grudgingly let me go.

There were several German women at the embassy hoping to immigrate to America. I overheard their chatter. Many of them were planning to marry Americans; others wanted to become *Kindermaedchen,* or nannies. When I joined the conversation, I told them about my cousin Rose and how she was going to sponsor me.

Then we were herded into a room and instructed to strip down to our underpants and bras. We waited around half-naked for a long time until a doctor finally arrived. We lined up so the doctor could probe our open mouths with a tongue depressor.

When it was my turn, I asked him, "Why did I have to get undressed for you to look down my throat?"

He grinned. "Next!" he said, and I left.

Several agonizing months went by before I found out my application had been approved. The year was 1961, which was almost a full year since I had met Rose in Hagen. Although I was unsure what to expect across the ocean, I was confident that I could start my life again with a clean slate. I gave my notice at work and had two more weeks to fulfill my contract. Frau Scheff, always the pessimist, said, "I still don't think you'll do it." But she was wrong.

I went to the travel agency to book a one-way flight to New York. The agent, a genial young man, tried to convince me that traveling by ship would be less expensive, but I was firm. "No," I said, "I'm making a big decision to leave my country forever. If I have a change of heart, I might be tempted to jump in the water."

The wide-eyed look on the agent's face almost made me burst out laughing. Without further advice, he booked my flight on the now-defunct Trans World Airlines.

Before I could go to America, I had one last thing to do. I had to make the rounds saying goodbye to my family. But first, I had to bid adieu to the Scheff family and my co-workers at the sweater factory.

The most difficult farewell involved Frau Schliebener, the housekeeper, who had been my closest friend. Her eyes were filled with a terrible sadness. We both realized we would probably never see each other again on this earth.

"I will miss you," I told her.

After a final hug, I left quickly, afraid my feelings would overwhelm me.

The parting between Inge and me was quite different. She was thrilled to have a friend in America whom she could visit someday. With a lighter heart, we promised to write to each other.

By now, I was a seasoned traveler. Still, I felt relieved when I was settled in the compartment of the train that would take me to Wilhelmshaven to say goodbye to all my family members.

I stayed with Ilse for a few days and planned to see my other siblings. I even called my father and his wife, Dora, and made arrangements to visit them. When I arrived, Dora was busy in the kitchen, and my father sat in front of a blaring television. He never bothered to turn off the TV, so our short conversation was permeated with loud background noise. His final comment always stuck with me.

"Well, good luck to you. At least you have a cousin there."

His lackluster farewell finally proved that he didn't care about me. I don't know what I expected him to say, but that bland, uncaring statement was worse than I imagined. After a firm handshake from

Dora, I shut the door and breathed a deep sigh of relief. I was done with my father!

Ilse had arranged for Traute and Guenter to be at her house to see me off. It was wonderful to see them, but I wondered when we would see each other again. The bittersweet reunion came to a close, and Ilse took me to the train station. I had mixed emotions running through my head: sadness for leaving my only flesh and blood behind, but happiness for a new beginning. I boarded the train after Ilse, shared a final handshake, and waved my white handkerchief from the window until we could no longer see each other. Mentally, I ticked off another obligation I had completed before starting my new life so far away from here. The train rattled toward Hagen while I tried to analyze my family. Perhaps the experience of surviving the war had scarred us forever.

I was glad no one spoke to me during the train ride. Everyone stared out the window or read the newspaper, while the monotonous clickity-clack made me drowsy. In spite of my heavy heart, I was still excited by the prospect of going to the United States.

At least I had my Tante Erna's smiling face to greet me when I arrived at Hagen. I hugged her and thanked her for meeting me at the station. As we piled my suitcases on a cart,

I noticed their number had increased since my last visit. The additional baggage was a result of my effort to accumulate a nice wardrobe. I was proud that I would be well-dressed in America.

A short taxi ride later, we were at their apartment. The first thing I noticed was the big smile on my Grandmother's face, showing her happiness for my return. She had aged since I last saw her. Perhaps her hair looked grayer in its twisted topknot, or maybe her weathered face added a wrinkle or two. Then I remembered how hard her life had been. I'm sure it had taken its toll.

The visit with Tante Erna and Oma passed slowly; I was too anxious to leave. Finally, as I rested my head on my pillow a final time, I thought, *"This is my last night of sleep in Germany."* My prayers that night were simple: I asked God to give me a peaceful rest and help me through tomorrow and thereafter.

Praying came a little easier for me. Living with Tante Erna and Oma influenced the beginning of my faith. Listening to their praying and reading scripture brought some meaning into my life, but I still didn't feel the same personal connection to God that they did. With the future ahead of me, I thought anything was possible. I finally fell asleep.

The next morning, the alarm clock rousted me out of bed. I could barely contain my excitement—the day was finally here! I dressed carefully in a pretty dress, made sure my bags were packed, and had a light breakfast with my aunt and grandmother.

Sipping a cup of tea, Tante Erna made a last attempt to keep me in Hagen. "Are you sure you don't want to stay with us?" she asked. "It's not too late to change your mind."

My silence was the only answer I could give her. I wasn't going to change my mind; the decision was final. As I hugged my grandmother, I wondered if I would ever see her alive again.

"I'll write soon," I promised.

Outside, the taxi honked. I had to go. Tante Erna accompanied me all the way to Frankfurt Airport. While waiting for my plane, the silence between us stretched uncomfortably. I just didn't want to talk. Subconsciously, I had already left my old life behind. When I heard the announcement to board my flight, I was relieved. Now, my journey begins! I thought.

I thanked my aunt for everything and promised to write as soon as I got there. She gave me a big hug and a kiss, then called out to me, "Say hello to Rose, Hjalmar, and little Roy."

I glanced over my shoulder to see her wipe the tears from her eyes.

At the gate, I checked in for my flight. As I sat down, I was introduced to my first culture shock. Everyone around me was speaking English! Although I was still on German soil, the people boarding my flight were, apparently, all Americans. Of course, my dictionary was in my suitcase, which was on its way to the belly of the plane. I smiled and forced myself to relax. America, here I come!

The plane ride was uneventful, and the language barrier posed no major problems. Fortunately, there were some Americans aboard who spoke German, and they were kind enough to help me.

The plane landed in the afternoon under a bright, blue sky. While standing in line for airport security, I tensed up as I scanned the area around me, desperately looking for Rose. What would I do if she weren't here? I finally saw her beyond the sliding glass doors that separated U.S. Customs from the public lobby. Getting through customs was a long, grueling process, and I spent the time battling my doubts. What have I done? How can I function in this country without speaking English? I decided to shelve my jittery nerves until after I spoke to Rose and her husband, Hjalmar.

Whoosh! The sliding doors opened. In the press of the crowd, I heard, "Gerda, we're over here!" I turned my head and spotted them instantly since they were both tall. Rose was five-foot-eight, and Hjalmar was well over six feet.

Their big, welcoming hugs were a tremendous comfort; it felt good to be around the people who would be my voice for a while.

"Let's get out of this huge crowd!" Rose said. She wore a black coat with a colorful scarf draped around her neck. Her brown hair, thick and curly, complemented the warm blue eyes that made me feel so welcome. Hjalmar was more reserved than his pretty wife. He had an oval face and dark blond hair. As soon as he spoke, his native Norwegian heritage became apparent. He was so tall he had to bend over a little to talk to me.

My host and hostess insisted we take a tour of the city before going to their home in Griggstown, New Jersey. Tired and hungry, I couldn't match their enthusiasm, but I didn't have the heart to say no.

The first few minutes in New York were overwhelming. The city was humongous, and everything I had read before couldn't compare with the real thing.

"Wow!" I said as I stared at the monumental buildings. They reminded me of a Steinwueste, a stone desert. My eyes simply could not take it all in.

The drive to Griggstown, which is near Princeton, stretched on and on, and I was eager to see the house that Rose and Hjalmar lived in. We drove on a country road for several miles before we finally made the last turn and pulled into the garage.

I was impressed with their home. Hjalmar built it himself a few years ago, so everything was new and inviting. How nice to have a handy and talented man for a husband. Rose always loved beautiful things, and their home was tastefully decorated with them. Instantly, I felt like I had come home.

Rose and Hjalmar were so kind and made me feel comfortable from the start. Deep in my heart, I realized this was the family I had been searching for. I was certain I would be able to leave Germany in the past, including all the heartaches and disappointments.

Hjalmar spoke German, which made communication between us so easy. Roy, who was seven now, remembered me from the year before.

He and I became good friends, and he started teaching me English. When we played games together, it was easy for me to pick up a lot of words. Roy was so adorable, and spending time with him reminded me of being with my little brothers.

Rose and Hjalmar were generous to let me stay with them for quite a while; nevertheless, I eventually knew I would have to strike out on my own.

—⁓⁓∘⌒⊙⌒⊙⌒⊙⌒∘⁓⁓—

Three months later, I awoke to hear the usual hustle and bustle of getting Roy off to school. I decided to linger in bed a little longer. Besides, I didn't want to be in the way. Drowsy with sleep, I mulled over my uncertain future. Why these fears hit me when I first opened my eyes every morning was unknown. Someday, a psychologist would have to unravel the mystery for me, but in the meantime, I thought, Maybe I'll stay here until Hjalmar leaves for work and Roy goes off to school. I turned over and dozed off again.

The aroma of coffee reawakened me. It was time to get up, no matter how comfortable Die Federbetten, the feather bed, was. My bed reminded me of the room I occupied while living in Scheff's house in Germany. I remember many nights when I collapsed into the comfortable featherbed after working hard at the factory all day. "Good morning, Rose," I said as I walked into the kitchen. "I hope you slept well." After the cheerful greeting, I blurted, "Ich muss mir Arbeit suchen, ja?" I need to find work, don't I?

Rose's simple shrug of her shoulders told me she agreed. I knew it was time to get serious about supporting myself. After all, I had promised. I broke the silence by asking Rose to take me to the nearest employment agency.

Rose drove me to the agency in New Brunswick, New Jersey. (Neither of us was aware that we didn't have to make the trip because the Help Wanted section in the newspaper would have been sufficient.) I wore a black-and-white-checkered suit and was self-confident in my outward professional appearance. On the inside, however, I was a wreck. I'm sure Rose was tired of my nervous chatter during the ride there. Poor thing, she tried to answer a barrage of questions, like: How old are these buildings? Is this neighborhood safe? Where are those people going?

At least my English had improved sufficiently enough to get a job. I could understand everything quite well; however, speaking was another matter. As long as I had German-speaking people around me, I didn't have to speak English. However, when I was forced to speak English, I was able to carry on a simple conversation.

As far as my employment was concerned, I had two choices: Either I could work in a factory, or I could become a nanny. My preference was the nanny position since I loved children. Another added benefit was learning more English by being around children. Unfortunately, there weren't any job openings for a nanny. I resigned myself to the drudgery of factory work.

Then the petite woman sitting behind the desk made an unexpected suggestion. "Would you be interested in helping an elderly couple in their home?"

Without any reservations, I nodded yes.

"You'll have to meet them first," the agent explained, "but that shouldn't be a problem."

The next morning, Rose and I enjoyed a quiet breakfast. As I sat there munching on my toast, I thought about how our lives would change if I got this job. We had fallen into the habit of watching late- night movies together after everyone else had gone to sleep. It didn't matter if the movie was terrible; we had to watch it to the end just to see what happened. Then we'd complain about how we wasted our time. Actually, I learned a lot by watching those bad movies. When I didn't understand something, Rose would explain it. My English might have improved, but my taste in the cinema didn't.

Now, as we lingered over our breakfast, I said, "I guess our late movie nights are over."

Rose reassured me, "They don't have to be. We'll find different times."

I smiled at her, grateful she took me into her heart like a sister.

"Are you ready for your interview with the Duncans?" she asked, pushing herself up from the chair and taking her dishes to the sink.

The Duncans were the elderly couple who needed my help. They lived in Highland Park, a half-hour ride from my own family. My own family! I liked how the words rolled off my tongue. My family lives in Griggstown, New Jersey. Yes, I definitely liked the sound of that.

Rose called and set up an interview for the following night.

The next evening, as Rose drove me to meet my prospective employers, I scrutinized the traditional homes lining the street and the abundance of old maple and oak trees in the yards of the Highland Park neighborhood. I pictured myself taking a leisurely stroll through the neighborhood, and the thought was nice.

Then we stopped in front of one of the lovely homes. My heart started racing as I wiped my sweaty palms on my lap. "Okay, Gerda," I mumbled to myself. "There's no turning back now."

Rose gave me a confident pat on the shoulder as she rang the doorbell.

Mrs. Duncan opened the door and shook our hands. She was a stunning, slender lady in her mid-sixties, and she wore her hair pulled back. "Please come in," she said, opening the door wider.

"This is my husband," she said, gesturing to the man sitting on the couch smoking his pipe.

Mr. Duncan extended his hand and smiled warmly. We started a pleasant chat to get acquainted, and I learned that Mr. Duncan was the president of a savings bank.

During the conversation, I couldn't help but notice their lovely home. My eyes soaked up the antique furniture and the lavish imported rugs. The room was both sumptuous and friendly, as was the rest of the house.

After a few minutes, we went up to the third floor to inspect my living quarters. Mr. Duncan pointed proudly to an air conditioner. "I went out last week and got it, especially for you because it does get a bit hot up here," he confided. The attic room didn't have the luxurious appointments found in the rest of the house, but it covered all the basics.

We agreed that I would start my job in a week's time. Rose and I were almost ready to leave when a young, handsome man entered the room.

"My name is Robert," he said, introducing himself. "I'm their son." He offered his hand to me. "I'm glad you'll be working here." His smile seemed friendly enough, and I appreciated the sincere welcome.

He continued, "I can teach you English, and you can teach me German."

On my first morning at work, I learned that one of my chores was fixing breakfast. Mrs. Duncan taught me how to make fried eggs, although my first attempt landed in the garbage. It was overcooked, and the edges were brown. I caught on quickly and only did that once.

Later that day, I discovered I would be required to wear a uniform. Much to my chagrin, I had to add a white apron to the outfit when serving dinner. Obviously, if I had to serve the meal, I wouldn't be eating with the family, so I had to take my meals in the kitchen alone. I quickly learned to despise the little bell Mrs. Duncan used to summon me. It was installed by her foot under the Oriental rug in the dining room. Several times during that first day, I wondered if I would have taken the job if I'd known all the rules.

When I went to bed that night, I was so unhappy about being a servant that I started to weep in my pillow. I guess I finally fell asleep because the next thing I remembered, it was morning. The sun shone so brightly that I felt a little better.

I'm glad I stuck it out. After I had been there for a while, I decided I liked Mr. Duncan a lot. For one thing, he was generous with his compliments toward me. Starved for praise, I liked it when he said, "You're a very smart girl." Whenever he did this, I thanked him and continued with my chores. The funny thing was, I didn't know what "smart" meant and was too embarrassed to ask him. One time, Robert was present when his father told me how smart I was. Robert caught on that I didn't understand what "smart" meant, so he bought me an English-German/German-English dictionary. I was overjoyed and thankful for this wonderful book—it was the first time I had received one as a gift. (Even today, as I recall that thoughtful gesture, my eyes well up with tears.)

The Duncans showered me with praise, and I absorbed their positive words like a sponge. I wish I had this affection while growing up, but at least I had these wonderful people in my life at that moment.

I settled into the daily routine of a servant, although I still didn't enjoy eating by myself or wearing a stupid uniform. As soon as I finished my job in the evenings, I went up to my room, changed my clothes, and went for a walk. It was a quiet, lonesome life, but over a four-month period, the added exercise caused me to lose almost twenty pounds, which I didn't miss one bit.

Robert was an attorney, and he commuted to his job in New York. But I liked it best when he was around. He made me laugh and took a genuine interest in building up my language skills; in fact, he convinced his parents to let me eat with them in the dining room so I could learn faster. It seemed counterproductive to wear a uniform while dining with them, so they dispensed with it altogether. Boy, was I glad!

Every morning, Mr. Duncan came down the stairs with his pipe in his mouth, wound the old grandfather clock, and greeted me heartily, "Good morning, Gerda!"

That friendly, familiar start to my day reinforced my opinion that the whole family was kind to me even though they didn't have to be.

Mr. Duncan also had an interesting hobby. He was an active ham radio operator, and sometimes, I listened to him as he chatted around the globe. His one limitation was only communicating with people who spoke English since he had no foreign language skills.

How I adored that old man! Secretly, I wished he were my father—how proud and thankful I would have been. I knew it was just a dream, but I guess it didn't hurt to have one.

One day, Mr. Duncan approached me out of the blue and asked, "Gerda, how would you like to go to a public school here in Highland Park?"

I was perplexed by his offer, but I liked the idea. I nodded, thinking, What a great opportunity to improve my English. To my surprise, it only took a couple of weeks before I joined a class of Highland Park sixth-graders. It felt strange. Here I was, twenty-three and sitting on the bench with twelve-year-olds, but the kids were kind to me, and the teachers treated me with respect.

I remember a particular assignment that the English teacher gave us. "I want a ten-minute speech on a famous dead person." Then he walked by my seat and gave me a helpful tip. "Read the newspaper," he whispered. "Eleanor Roosevelt just died."

I nodded and smiled.

Two weeks later, it was my turn to speak. I remember standing at the head of the class and waiting for everyone to settle down. I heard a hushed cough from the back of the room. The institution-green walls absorbed the hum of the fluorescent lights above, and I began my speech. When I finished, I was proud of my performance. Then I threw my arms in the air and said, "That's all, folks." The kids laughed, and I was relieved it was over.

But times have changed. Today, it wouldn't be acceptable for a twenty-three-year-old to register for middle school. Not only would the students not accept it, I doubt the school administration would allow it. I don't remember how long I attended classes, but I still have my first report card, and it was a good one.

———⁓⊱⋅⊱◈⊰⋅⊰⁓———

Robert's sister, Nancy Seibert, and her husband, Tom lived next door to the Duncans. Nancy, another kind soul who took an interest in me, brought me magazines to improve my reading skills. Tony, their teenage son, had little interest in the lady next door struggling with the language. The only reason I mention this at all is because

Nancy and I have stayed in contact over the years, even if it's only greetings at Christmastime. She lives in a retirement community in Highland Park.

Life with the Duncan family continued to shape my existence. They introduced me to their friends and sometimes took me out to dinner. I have many fond memories of these occasions since the couple entertained often.

On one occasion, they invited me as a guest to their catered party. I bought a lovely dress, wore pretty shoes, and put on makeup. Then the guests arrived. I came halfway down the stairs and froze. My eyes darted around the room, and I realized how well-educated all these people were with big, important jobs. I had nothing in common with them. My palms were sweaty, my heart was racing, and my face was beet red. Looking back, I suppose I experienced a full-blown panic attack. All I could think about was escaping back to my room and staying put.

Mrs. Duncan knocked on my door and tried to coax me out. "Please, Gerda, come down. Our friends would like to meet you." Her plea failed to change my mind. I just couldn't do it. The next day, nobody said anything, and thankfully, my behavior at the party never came up again.

Most of Mrs. Duncan's friends ran in high society circles. Among them were the Thompsons, who had close ties to Johnson & Johnson, a household corporate name in the United States. One beautiful, sunny afternoon, Mrs. Duncan took me to the Thompsons' home for tea. Coming up the driveway, I admired their beautiful estate overlooking the Raritan River.

For all their wealth, the Thompsons never treated me like a maid. In fact, Mr. and Mrs. Thompson picked me up at the Duncans' home and took me to dinner. It was such a lovely evening, and it strengthened my opinion that these people gave "class" a good name.

Robert enjoyed watching live sports and often invited me to go with him. I thoroughly enjoyed the hockey games at Princeton, his alma mater. I'm not a huge sports fan, but hockey was easy to figure out: two teams, two goals, one puck. One team tries to get the puck into the other team's goal and vice versa.

Baseball, on the other hand, was a different story. I'll never forget the first time he took me to a baseball game. I had absolutely no clue about how the sport was played, and I can't believe I actually sat through a double-header.

I do know that I loved being with Robert. Perhaps I even fell in love with him, and that was a scary prospect for me. Becoming a wife and having my own children was my fondest wish, and socializing with him probably fueled that desire because he was such a wonderful guy.

I think it was around 1963 when Mr. and Mrs. Duncan suggested I should get my driver's license.

"It would help my wife tremendously," Mr. Duncan reasoned. "Then you could take Robert to the train station in the mornings and pick him up when he comes home in the evenings." Obviously, any excuse to hang around Robert was fine by me.

A few days later, on a Saturday afternoon, the two men decided it was time to give me my first driving lesson. Robert put me behind the steering wheel, and he sat in the passenger seat. After Mr. Duncan climbed into the backseat, off we went.

The streets were deserted as he directed me around the block. I carefully maneuvered the car down the wide road, secretly pleased that I seemed to be a natural. All of a sudden, he yelled, "Hit the brakes!" There was no emergency; he was just testing my reflexes. I felt like screaming back at him, but I didn't. Robert barked out a few more commands, and the next thing I knew, I was driving down Main Street, handling the traffic like a pro. Mr. Duncan shook his head from the backseat. "You amaze me, Gerda," he said. "You make it look so easy."

On my days off, Rose picked me up so we could spend the whole day together. I had so much to tell her and so many questions to ask. The best thing, though, was that I could speak German with her.

When she found out that I wanted to get my driver's license, she took me to the Motor Vehicle Bureau to pick up the instruction manual. I studied it, and two weeks later, I took the written test and passed it.

I suppose my pride was clearly written on my face—I had a grin a mile wide as I handed the temporary license to Robert. He teased, "So you got your smiler's license, huh?" Mr. Duncan was also pleased with my accomplishment and made a point of congratulating me. I thought I deserved a little more recognition from Robert than his smart remark, so I figured out a way to get him back.

"Robert," I asked, "do you really want to know how I passed so easily?"

He shrugged his shoulders, so I continued.

"I wore a tight skirt and a sexy sweater for the test. During the exam, I dropped my pencil, and when I was sure the examiner was looking at me, I swung my hips as I picked it up."

The entire Duncan family was speechless, but at least I got my point across to Robert.

Mr. Duncan generously offered his car for my driving test. "I've ordered a new family car, but since you're used to driving this one, I'll keep it until you pass your test," he said.

Two weeks later, I passed my driving test with flying colors. Now, I wanted the freedom of owning my own vehicle. I had been frugal for a while, hoping to save enough money to get a used car, and I even knew which one I wanted. Hjalmar went with me to buy a Volkswagen, more commonly referred to as a "Beetle" or a "Bug." The army-green car was affordable and familiar, and I loved it.

———〰〰०ॐ✕⊙⊙✕ॐ०॰〰〰———

Robert took it upon himself to teach me the correct pronunciation of the English language, especially the "th" sound. It can be difficult for Germans to master because there isn't any such sound in our language. If I didn't pronounce "Mr. Smith" with my tongue between my teeth, Robert refused to take me to the movies. Another letter I found difficult to grasp was the "r" sound. He explained that I had to curl the back of my tongue up to make the sound properly. At night, I would lie in my bed and practice these sounds until I could say them perfectly.

Surviving through the winter months proved to be quite challenging. The dark evenings were lonely, and the dismal weather diminished my desire for walks. Often, I studied and read in my room. The nation had not become avid television watchers during that time, although the Duncans had a TV set in their study. Occasionally, Mr. Duncan invited me to watch a show with them. They also introduced me to the game of bridge, and soon, I was fascinated and serious about it. I don't remember how well I did, but I thoroughly enjoyed the game and continued to play through the years. Even today, I still relish the competition.

One morning, Mr. Duncan sat me down, and the serious expression on his face signaled an important matter.

"Gerda," he said, "I think you're ready to get your General Educational Development certification, a high school equivalency. I'd like to offer you a job at the bank. I talked with the other directors, and they all agree you could work during the day while you study for your GED in the evening."

I was stunned but, at the same time, flattered that he thought so highly of me. How ironic that my father took me out of school when I was fourteen and scoffed at the chance to better myself through education while this man, who owed me nothing, looked out for my educational development. Mr. Duncan was so generous that I never had to ask for his help. Knowing how grateful I was for the opportunity to better myself, he patted my shoulder lightly and said, "We'll go together and get you enrolled."

After I started my job at the bank, I felt it was time to move out of the Duncans' home. I liked the idea of being independent, but it was hard to say goodbye to the people who treated me like family. Robert reassured me, "I'm sure my parents want to stay in touch with you." I know his words were meant to calm me, but I picked up on the fact that he didn't mention his intentions to see me.

An ad in the newspaper directed me to a nice, affordable apartment. It was in the home of an elderly couple who allowed me to access their telephone, which saved me money. The modest salary I earned at the bank covered my rent, car insurance, and gas for my Volkswagen.

Occasionally, Mr. and Mrs. Duncan asked me to dinner at their house. It was nice to visit with them, but their invitation meant Robert could see me without having to make a date.

My English was progressing, my job at the bank was going well, and I continued to pursue my diploma at the local high school. As I became more engrossed with my new life, I saw the Duncans less often—I missed them, especially Robert.

On the other hand, I made new friends at school. I became close to Helga, a pretty German girl with a wonderful sense of humor. Helga and I often studied after school and spent time together on the weekends. She lived close to me and often invited me out with her boyfriend, John, a medical student. I wished I had taken them up on their offer to go out and have fun, but I opted to stay home in case Robert called. Perhaps I read more into our relationship than was there. Instead of discussing it with him, I assumed the worst and decided to move on.

Rose and her family were a great comfort, and they helped ease the disappointment.

Full of despair and disappointment, I tried to wipe Robert's memory from my mind, but it cost me many restless nights. Often, I fell asleep out of sheer exhaustion.

Imagine my surprise when he called to invite me to a Princeton football game.

I was thrilled… for a moment. The next sentence crushed my dream: One of his New York lady friends would accompany him, and he set me up with a blind date. I wondered if this arrangement was his way of telling me our friendship would not develop into a serious relationship.

I decided to take him up on his offer anyway. A night out in the town would break up my work and school routines. Now, I focused on looking my best. As I slipped my new coat over my new dress, I was pleased with my reflection in the mirror.

Robert picked me up and introduced me to my blind date, a charming New York gentleman who was a stockbroker. My confused expression prompted Robert to explain.

"A stockbroker sells shares," he said.

I mistook the word "shares" for "chairs," so I thought my

date was a furniture salesman.

Arriving in Princeton, New Jersey, Robert introduced me to Kenneth, his former college roommate. Unfamiliar with this kind of American living arrangement, I thought he said "room maid," which didn't make any sense to me.

The football game was uneventful, and my memory of it is sketchy at best. Then, we all met back in a student meeting room, where the ladies spread their mink coats on the floor. The men supplied the liquor, and we had a drink or two.

I felt so out of place. The language barrier became more apparent, and I didn't possess their natural confidence and ease. So, I remained silent.

I didn't think the evening could get much worse, but it did. The plan was to have dinner in New York, so we all piled into the car to make the trip from Jersey. I was wedged in the middle of the backseat, and the uncomfortable ride seemed endless. Again, I couldn't take part in their easy banter, and I sat there like a statue.

Finally, we made it to New York. Since our reservations were for a later time, we decided to have a quick cocktail at Kenneth's apartment, which was in close proximity to the restaurant.

When we arrived, a butler whisked our coats away with silent efficiency. My eyes swept around the room, taking in the expansive space. The large apartment was beautifully furnished and decorated.

The butler began mixing drinks from an elegant sideboard. While we waited, Kenneth summoned the nanny to show off his children. Soon, a petite woman appeared with three children. The five-year-old boy was the oldest and might have been a handsome child except for the thick glasses perched on

111

his nose. I felt sorry for the middle one; she wore braces on her legs. I couldn't tell if the infant was a boy or a girl, but I was heartened to hear happy gurgling noises. Five minutes later, the nanny shuffled the children off to bed.

Although everyone was gracious toward me, I was terrified to speak. I would have loved to join in the conversation, but my heart throbbed at the thought of drawing attention to myself. It was quite obvious that Robert's friends were wealthy and comfortable with their social status.

After a few drinks, we left for the restaurant. Clearly, the establishment was geared toward the privileged few—dim lights surrounded the patrons who spoke in refined murmurs, and the intimate tables tucked here and there were graced with fine linens, elegant china, and sparkling crystal. Even the air smelled like old money.

I was told to order anything I wanted from the menu, but I was so taken with my surroundings that I couldn't tell you what I ate that long-ago night. By now, I just wanted to go home and crawl into bed.

The evening finally came to an end, and Robert and I bid farewell to his friends. I made sure to thank everyone for a lovely time. On the way home, we didn't talk much. That was fine with me because I didn't want to admit that most of the conversation went right over my head. I also realized my heavy German accent didn't fit well in upper-class America. Sleep evaded me for a long time that night, but I remember wishing I had been born here with all the advantages of the people I met that evening.

Almost three years had passed since that awkward night, but my language skills were improving, and so was my life.

Of course, my incomplete mastery of the English language still got me in trouble.

I remember the time I had to ask one of the bank managers a complicated question about tax statements. Carefully, I formulated my words and sentences the night before so I wouldn't be so flustered or nervous. I walked up to Mr. Williams and asked if I could interrupt him.

He replied, "Well, that is the prerogative of your sex." After I asked my question, he was able to clarify my concerns. Satisfied, I thanked him and turned to leave. Before I took a step, he called out, "Do you know what the phrase 'prerogative of your sex' means?"

"Of course I do. It means you always have time for sex." To my embarrassment, everyone burst out laughing.

Mr. Williams said, "I think you'd better go back for more English classes."

Actually, I was able to learn a lot of business English by listening to the other bank tellers. I studied what they asked the customers and listened to their answers.

My entire world at the time revolved around my job, school, and visiting my cousin Rose. Even though I was determined not to set myself up for rejection, I secretly wished Robert would call to ask me to go out. I even tried to date other men, but they didn't have his charm or sense of humor. I missed being around the Duncans, too.

I submerged myself in schoolwork to avoid being restless. I usually enjoyed the learning process, but one of my teachers was making me uncomfortable. Mr. Levine, my American history teacher, was Jewish. It was only from watching movies and documentaries in the United States that I learned of the terrible Nazi crimes against Jews. After that, I became tremendously insecure around a Jewish person, and Mr. Levine seemed to enjoy my discomfort. Eventually, I hated going to his class; I felt that uncomfortable. So, I quit and resolved to repeat the class with a different teacher.

Slowly, I forgot about my life in Germany. It wasn't that difficult since letters from my family and friends became less frequent. I made it a point not to dwell on the past; I worked and lived for the future. Although Americans were nice and friendly, very few made the effort to get to know me. The key to my success was getting more comfortable with the language.

Then Ida Lipp came into my life, and once again, my life changed course. I remember the day I ran into her—literally—on the street. I was walking briskly to my job one drizzling morning, and she was scampering toward an awning to stay dry. Neither one of us was paying attention, and we bumped into each other.

"*Entschuldigung!*" she said. Sorry!

My ears picked up my native tongue. "Are you all right?"

We chatted for a few minutes before I had to run off to work. I discovered she was visiting a relative but was originally from Munich, Germany. She now lived in Massachusetts, where she worked for the Massachusetts Institute of Technology. We exchanged telephone numbers and agreed to meet for coffee later that day.

We became fast friends; whether it was a common kinship or her bubbly personality, I don't know. Ida constantly raved about Boston, where she lived, and often mentioned how many eligible bachelors lived there too. Intrigued by her stories, I decided to see for myself.

I asked for a week's vacation and drove my VW up to

Boston. I stayed with Ida, who was looking for a roommate and eager for me to move in with her. I thought, Why not? I realized my life was getting stale, and I was ready for a change. I also knew that the first thing I had to do was find a job.

The next morning, I took the subway—which was a new experience for me—to downtown Boston. Emerging from the underground, I saw a sign that said Charlestown Savings Bank. Gathering up my courage, I went in and spoke to the manager. I explained to him that I was working in New Jersey and was planning to move to Boston. After a short, impromptu interview, he hired me. We negotiated a salary and agreed that I could start in two weeks.

I spent a few more days exploring the beautiful city I would soon call home. Yet another chapter of my life waited to be written, and I was anxious for it to start.

As I drove my green VW back to New Jersey, I had five hours to wonder if I had made the right choice. If Robert wanted to build a life with me, he would find a way to keep me there. If not, then it would have been better for everyone if I had moved on.

Mr. and Mrs. Duncan invited me to their house one day to hear about my vacation. I told them about my new job in Boston and my two-week departure. Besides being kind and gentle, Mr. Duncan was a perceptive man. With a wink, he voiced his opinion. "Don't give up on Robert," he said. "You know, my wife and I would welcome you into the family with open arms."

Although it was reassuring to hear him speak on behalf of his son, I had to hear those words from Robert. However, I knew the truth: my dysfunctional German family and lack of a college education would always be stumbling blocks for him. A life with him was my dream, not his.

During my last two weeks in New Jersey, Robert was away on vacation and made it a point not to call or say goodbye. I packed up my belongings and moved on with unresolved issues trailing behind me.

All my possessions went into my car. As I drove away, tears of self-doubt cut a shiny path down my cheeks. I was tired of saying goodbye to my friends and family, although Rose and Hjalmar understood why I needed to go. Leaving Mr. Duncan behind in my past was hard. I sensed he was especially sad to see me go.

Ida and I got along well as roommates, and soon, I was meeting lots of young people. True to her word, there were many eligible bachelors around, and Ida and I dated a few MIT and Harvard guys. I was careful about my reputation, though. My old friend, Dr. Kleber, warned me a long time ago about men taking advantage of German girls.

I adjusted quickly to my new surroundings. I loved my job, attending cultural events, and double-dating with Ida. All in all, life was good. Every once in a while, I hoped Robert would call or visit me, but I refused to dwell on the past.

My ambition to finish the American history class surfaced once again. A few more English credits wouldn't hurt either, so I enrolled myself in night classes at MIT. How fun it was to brag that I was attending that prestigious institution.

After six months of working at the bank, I received my first evaluation. Raises were awarded based on how accurate, efficient, and punctual we were. Since I worked hard, I excelled in all areas. It didn't take long before I was promoted to a personal banker. Full of pride and ambition, I was ready to move up in the banking field.

One of my many duties was opening up new accounts. I

remember the time when Mr. and Mrs. Goldstein sat across my desk. They peered at my nameplate, and I'm sure the name "Gerda Hartwich" disclosed my German heritage. Why did I feel such shame when I had to serve Jewish people? I personally didn't cause them pain, although I wondered if the Goldsteins had suffered in any direct way resulting from Hitler's evil tyranny. There was a compulsion deep within my soul to apologize for the Holocaust, but I never spoke the words. Instead, I made sure I served them with great respect.

The time came when I finally finished all my high school classes, and it felt rewarding to have that behind me. With extra time on my hands, Ida and I added more activities to our social lives, such as going to the theater, skating, and playing tennis. I took a few tennis lessons, and when I had nothing else to do, I went to the high school and practiced my shots on the backboard. (Little did I know that smashing tennis balls into the backboard would be therapy for my future mental health. Back then, I was happy to improve my game.) One day, Ida suggested we visit three bachelors she knew down the street. Apparently, their apartment complex had a laundry room in the basement, and she thought that would be better than going to the Laundromat.

Usually ready for an adventure, I agreed. We stuffed our laundry in pillowcases, slung them over our shoulders like Santa Claus, and shuffled down the street to their apartment. I rang the doorbell and was greeted by a nice-looking young man named Dallas Robinson. My heart thumped a little as we chatted. I discovered he had graduated from Harvard Business School and worked for IBM. His job would soon be transferring him to Burlington, Vermont, and I felt a twinge of sadness. Our laundry chores were over, and we left.

That evening, when I went to bed, my thoughts came back to him. It's too bad this nice guy I just met would be out of my life.

Several months had passed, and I quickly forgot about Dallas Robinson. When October 7—my birth date—rolled around, I was surprised to get a letter from him. How did he know it was my birthday? Of course, he didn't—the arrival of his letter was a coincidence. Still, it was a nice "present," and I pored over it eagerly.

He invited me to a Harvard-Princeton football game to help him cheer on the Harvard team. Unexpectedly, Robert had called a few days earlier, inviting me to the same football game. I chose to cheer for Princeton. I called Dallas and told him I wasn't available, but I looked forward to seeing him in the future.

It did my heart good to see Robert again. I was able to see his true character for the first time. I still loved his sense of humor, but there was one personality flaw I couldn't overlook: he was too concerned about what other people thought.

I would always be indebted to him for introducing me to so many new and different ideas and experiences, but that didn't make him the right person to spend a life with. I remembered how he always criticized my English, and I realized how his close scrutiny caused my self-esteem to plummet.

No, he wasn't the right person for me. Taking this hard, honest look at our relationship freed my heart forever. It felt good to tie up that loose end in my life.

Thank goodness Dallas didn't give up on me! Several weeks later, he invited me to a party that his former roommates had at their apartment. I was touched that he made the long drive down to see me. I guess this marked the beginning of our

118

courtship.

As Christmas drew closer, Dallas mentioned that he was going back to his hometown of St. Louis, Missouri, for the holidays. I wonder what he told his family about me. All I remember is that once he was there, he called to let me know how happy his family was that he found "the one." That's when I sensed things might be getting serious between us—that we might build a life together.

As our relationship blossomed, I was grateful that Dallas didn't ask too many questions about my family. When I did mention them, I didn't get too specific about the unpleasant details. After all, I had traveled three thousand miles to forget my life in Germany, to leave behind the painful memories of my family, especially my father.

I shared the news about the new young man in my life with Rose and Hjalmar. She was worried that at my ripe old age of twenty-six, I would be marked as an old maid forever.

Dallas and I continued to stay in touch by phone and letters, and our commitment grew stronger.

"It'll be Easter soon," Dallas wrote in one of his special letters. "I plan on coming down to Boston. Would you consider going to church with me on Sunday?"

I was overjoyed by the prospect of going to church with him, especially during a religious holiday.

Easter arrived, and he drove down from Burlington to take me to church as promised. After the service, we drove to New Jersey so he could meet my cousin and her family. The sunny day filled my heart, and we all had a wonderful time. I watched Dallas play with James, Rose, and Hjalmar's newest addition to the family. They rolled around in the grass for a while, and Dallas proved to be a natural with children. It was nice to know he had great paternal instincts; that was important to me.

On the way back home, he mentioned his family was coming to Boston in June, and they were looking forward to meeting me. What if I don't like them? I thought. Perhaps they won't accept me. These uneasy thoughts rolled around my head so long that I had to force them away.

The day Dallas proposed was on a sunny Saturday, the kind of day God created for special events: the air was sweet and clean, the skies were clear and bright, and life seemed full of wonderful possibilities. When Dallas arrived for our date, he looked so handsome in his suit. I was bursting with pride to be seen on his arm.

The dinner at Jimmy's Harborside restaurant in Boston was delicious, and we enjoyed each other's company while gazing out over the water. On the drive back to Cambridge, however, he suggested a walk by the river. By now, dusk had blanketed the once-bright day.

The warm breeze rustled the branches overhead, soothing my soul. I heard a couple whispering to each other while sitting on a park bench. We must have chased them away because they disappeared into the silky darkness as we approached.

He guided me to the now-empty bench, and we sat there together in the calm evening, enjoying each other's company. I felt the excitement in the air but was unaware of the source.

He grasped my hand and asked, "Will you marry me?"

I almost burst with joy. "Yes!" I replied, not hesitating for a second. Actually, I had planned on saying yes for quite some time. I knew he was the right man for me. He was smart, polite, gentle, and kind.

Most importantly, he accepted me as I was. The mere thought of becoming part of his family was more than I had dreamed of for a long time. He wanted to give me an engagement ring right away, but I suggested meeting his family before I had the ring on my finger.

"Whatever makes you comfortable," he said in his gentle voice. With much trepidation, the day finally arrived when I would meet my future in-laws. Why did the day have to be so cold and dreary?

We were meeting his parents at a restaurant in Swampscott, Massachusetts. Dallas picked me up, and I had gone to great lengths to make sure I looked my best. I must have tried on several outfits before I settled on the beautiful red dress I wore. The classic lines flattered my figure, but the vibrant color added a touch of glamour.

My thoughts were racing so fast that it was impossible for me to remain calm. I would have considered a stiff drink to bolster my courage, but it was too early in the morning.

As we entered the restaurant, my eyes swept the room until I saw them sitting in the corner. My future mother-in-law came toward me and shook my hand.

"I've been looking forward to meeting you for some time now!" Her warm, friendly greeting put me at ease.

His father, a prominent businessman in St. Louis, came across a little cold. Meeting the rest of the family was easier. His sister Susan, an attractive young woman, shook my hand first, then her daughter Michele, a cute four-year-old. Stephen, Dallas's younger brother, was the last one to greet me.

The meal was pleasant enough, although I can't remember one thing I ate. I also have little recollection about the décor or if the place was busy or not. I was glad that our conversation remained casual—nothing too deep or personal. The only awkward moment occurred when my future father-in-law asked, "And what do you do for the bank?"

I felt embarrassed because I didn't have a fancy title to impress him. I mentioned the job in the mortgage department that was offered to me; I had declined since I knew I would be moving to Vermont with Dallas soon.

At that point, my wonderful husband-to-be came to my rescue and recited every one of my accomplishments since coming to this country five years ago.

Dallas's brother Stephen seemed nice, although the handsome twenty-four-year-old was relatively quiet. I later learned that he had schizophrenia.

I figured Dallas's sister to be around my age. I didn't know it at the time, but she was going through a divorce; perhaps that was the reason she didn't say much.

The above photo is from our wedding but offers images of the people I met that day, except for his grandmother, who was not present in Swampscott. Left to right in the photo are Dallas's father (Carl), sister (Susan), niece (Michele, Susan's daughter), me, Dallas, his grandmother (Nellie Bennett), Dallas's mother (Dorothy), and his brother (Steve).

After the meal, we roamed around the city for a few hours, and then his family went home. I was glad that the meeting was over, but I could tell they all liked and accepted me. Shortly after that, Dallas placed an engagement ring on my finger. The next step was planning a wedding.

By the end of 1966, I knew we were going to St. Louis for Christmas. At first, getting married the next month— January— seemed like a good idea. To save some of the expense of making two trips to St. Louis, we also discussed the possibility of having the wedding in New Jersey, but Dallas had lots of aunts, uncles, and cousins, and it would be a long way for them to travel.

His mother wanted a large wedding, which would have meant two hundred guests or more. So, after a long discussion, we came up with a compromise. We would have the ceremony in St. Louis in December rather than making a separate trip in January. And so it happened that we were married on Saturday, December 31, 1966.

There were only twenty-eight guests present, mostly family members and a few friends. His mother was slightly disappointed by not getting the extravagant event she wanted, but it was a lovely day. Even though I didn't know most of the people at my own ceremony, I didn't feel like a stranger at all.

We spent our honeymoon in Nassau, Bahamas, and I was delighted to hear everyone call me "Mrs. Robinson." Not only did I have a wonderful new husband, but I finally had my very own family. Even his parents insisted I call them Mom and Dad, and I accepted that request with great pleasure.

Our first address as husband and wife was Dallas's upstairs bachelor apartment in Burlington, Vermont, but after a few months, we moved to a lovely first-floor apartment. From our living room, big sliding doors opened onto a beautiful courtyard. Our spectacular view included the birch trees, lush grass, and a multitude of colorful flowers.

I started to settle into our life together. Dallas returned to work at IBM, and I took care of the house. I felt at peace and thanked God for my new surroundings; it was the perfect setting for the promise of our first child.

CHAPTER 6
FINALLY, A FAMILY OF MY OWN

Dallas's mother, Dorothy, was thrilled with the expectation of her second grandchild, and she visited us often. I welcomed these trips because I loved having a "real" mother in my life. She never complained about the arduous journey; she never criticized me or made me feel inadequate. Dorothy accepted me unconditionally. I was thankful we had forged a mother/daughter bond between us, especially since I heard little from the old country.

The focus of my life centered on taking care of my husband and our home while awaiting the birth of our child. On August 27, 1967, our daughter Kim entered the world, but she sure took her time getting here.

The first time I felt a sharp pain was on a Friday evening, and my husband was still at the office. Dallas rushed home immediately after receiving my call. He probably ran a few red lights while speeding home because it didn't take him long to arrive. Then we hurried to the hospital. Diagnosis: false alarm.

The doctor wanted to induce labor the next morning, and I struggled with labor pains nearly all day. But the baby wasn't ready to join the outside world yet. By that evening, the doctors were afraid I might not have enough strength to deliver the next day. I got a dose of medicine that would allow me to rest for the night.

Finally, on Sunday afternoon at 3:00 p.m., Kim was born. The first time I held that sweet baby girl, I forgot all about the pain. As Dallas and I gazed at our precious child, we were happy that we had started a family. Truly, babies are God's greatest miracles.

For about a year and a half, I stayed busy with raising our daughter. Then in 1969, Dallas's parents desperately needed our help. His father had slipped deeper into alcoholism, and his mother couldn't cope anymore. She felt so helpless that she became depressed.

Dallas's grandmother, who owned an antique shop, was getting weaker and could no longer operate the business on her own. His sister Susan was recently divorced again, and she needed emotional support and help with her now-six-year-old daughter Michele.

The one family member who did not need help at the moment was his brother Steve. Diagnosed with schizophrenia, Steve was in the care of a psychiatrist, and his medication and treatment had been going well.

The family that I sought out so desperately now needed me. It was my turn to be their source of strength. My childhood taught me to be strong enough to survive. I was experienced in holding things together. Now that we were needed, Dallas and I planned to rearrange our lives to accommodate our St. Louis family.

Fortunately, Dallas's strong work ethic was an asset to IBM. The company valued his employment and readily allowed him to transfer to their office in St. Louis. It took a few weeks to organize the move from Vermont to Missouri, but the Robinson family was packed up and ready to go. Dallas and I, with our 18-month-old daughter, headed for St. Louis.

The move was easy, but we needed to find a home quickly. Thank goodness finding a home in America was easier than in Germany.

Where I was born, people usually stayed put; people in the United States buy and sell houses more frequently than Germans buy furniture.

Dallas's family lived in Webster Groves, a suburb of St. Louis. Many of the homes in this historic area were at least 100 years old. My mother-in-law, anxious for us to be near them, had already picked out a house for us across the street. But we thought that was a bit too close for comfort, so we opted for a place in Grantwood, about ten miles away. This beautiful development was in close proximity to a historic farm that was once owned by Ulysses S. Grant.

I'm sure Dorothy would have preferred we live on the same street; still, she was happy that we were here. We became good friends, and I found it easy to be with her. Grateful to be a part of the family, I became the pillar for everyone to lean on. Adept at caring for others, I didn't think to care for myself. But who knew that I needed to? For the time being, the general consensus was that we're glad Gerda is so strong.

My husband settled into his new life without difficulty since he grew up there, and he was pleased to be reunited with his family. He also reconnected with the St. Louis Philharmonic Orchestra, where he had played French horn since junior high school.

The job at IBM was demanding, so I welcomed this musical outlet to balance out his life. I also made sure he didn't have many household duties, so I cut the lawn, clipped the bushes, and painted the walls.

Meanwhile, I found out I was expecting our second child. Welcoming another addition to the family made me happy, but I was concerned about my health. I wasn't as well and strong as I wanted to be.

The pregnancy progressed smoothly. Then, early in the morning of October 20, I shook my husband awake at 5 o'clock.

"I'm having contractions," I said.

In a sleepy voice, he said, "Tell me when they get stronger."

By 7 a.m., I called the doctor. She didn't think I needed to rush to the hospital, so she told me to come in at 10 o'clock in the morning, which was my original appointment.

While rushing around to get my daughter ready to stay with her grandma, my water broke. I stopped long enough to put a pad inside my underwear, but I had to keep moving. Three hours later, we pulled into the hospital right on.

After signing in, I was wheeled into the labor room. My doctor stopped by to do a routine check, but her face was full of concern. "I can't hear a heartbeat," she said.

Once again, I needed God's help. Although my relationship with Him still wasn't on solid ground, I found solace when I prayed. The doctor told us to prepare ourselves for the worst, so I prayed a little harder.

After seven hours of hard labor, our son Carl was born. My arms ached to hold him, but his health problems wouldn't permit it. Two long days later, the nurse finally placed my beautiful son in my arms. "Thank you, dear Lord, for letting him live," I murmured into his little ear.

After a couple of days, we were allowed to go home. The doctor told me, "You'll know if something is wrong with him, but don't look for problems."

I trusted the doctor and God.

When our minister, Dr. Tucker, came to visit me, I mentioned my concerns about the baby's health, especially about Carl's lungs and heart.

Dr. Tucker's response frightened me. "The types of issues he had would most likely affect his brain."

Terrified, I called my pediatrician. "Your minister isn't a medical doctor. He shouldn't have said that," he said. Although the doctor tried to reassure me that our son was healthy, I could not shake the fear about his brain being damaged. Again, I had to trust God's will.

I just loved little Carl, who was such a happy baby, and I counted my blessings whenever I tucked those two precious children into bed. My lifelong prayers had been answered, and it turned out that my worries were unfounded.

Our son was named after my father-in-law. Dallas and I wanted to honor Dad by naming his first grandson after him. Perhaps a desire to live up to the honor would curb his appetite for alcohol. How little we understood his illness. Nothing changed; in fact, he began to drink even more.

Many long and busy days passed. One morning, I was sitting in our family room when I felt a sharp pain around my heart. Soon, the pain occurred once or twice a week, which frightened me. An awful thought ran through my head: Who would take care of my children if something happened to me? My newfound family had too many problems to take on another responsibility.

Besides, Mom's health had declined considerably, and she was going to the doctor more often. At one point, cancer was suspected, but the doctor eventually ruled it out. Still, she underwent several abdominal surgeries, and during one of them, the doctors removed a large section of her colon, more than they anticipated. Three months later, she needed another surgery.

While Mom was recuperating at home, Dad, Dallas, and I looked after her mother, Grandma Bennett, who lived with them in Webster Groves. Every morning, Dad took her with him on his way to work and dropped her off at her antique store in the Old Gaslight Square District in St. Louis. She couldn't manage the large shop on her own, and we tried to convince her to move and downsize. Too committed to her independence, she refused.

The pain around my heart became unbearable, and I finally admitted it to my doctor. He asked me about my daily routine and came to the conclusion that I needed Valium. So, every night, I took my pill. I was relieved when the pain went away, and I could do everything that was necessary to care for the family.

Finding time for myself was not easy. Once a month, I managed to squeeze in a tennis match, but that was it. I also stole a few moments out of the house when a friend and I would set up the playpen and visit while our children played together.

Life rolled on. Dallas worked hard and played his French horn. Every Wednesday night, he was at orchestra rehearsal, and on Sunday nights, he played woodwind music at the home of Max Risch, the orchestra's principal bassoon player. My husband's passion for music excluded me. He wasn't around when I needed help or companionship, and I almost became resentful of the family I had wanted so much. But soon, the hectic pace of my life would catch up, and I would be too busy to spend time worrying about being resentful.

I was also too busy worrying about Mom. I remember one

130

Sunday evening when I wanted to visit her in the hospital because her most recent surgery hadn't gone well. Dad stayed home to drink, and my husband was at his friend's house playing in the horn quartet. I really wanted to be with Mom, so I called my babysitter. She was a godsend; she made herself available anytime I needed her.

As soon as I arrived at the hospital, I heard her shallow breathing.

I knew that my dear Dorothy was not doing well. She clung to my hand and started saying nonsensical things. "Oh, Gerda, it's beautiful here," she said. "I see white curtains blowing in the wind and beautiful flowers everywhere."

I didn't know if she was hallucinating, so I called the nurse to let her know that something was seriously wrong. Then I called my father-in-law and recommended that someone should stay through the night. I had children to care for, so I had to go home. The solution was to hire a special nurse to watch over her.

The following morning, Mom was placed in the Intensive Care Unit, where she was hooked up to every machine available. She tried to speak, but she lost her voice. I was able to read her lips. "I love you," she mouthed. For the next two days, we stayed vigilant at the hospital. Dallas spent both nights sleeping on a couch in the lobby. We were allowed five minutes of visitation every two hours.

On Tuesday morning, May 15, 1970, Dallas came into our bedroom and fell into my arms, weeping. Our dear mother was gone.

The doctor said the cause of death was liver failure due to the multitude of medications she had to take. How ironic that the pills that were supposed to keep her alive had actually

131

poisoned her system. Dallas and I were heartbroken, and I already missed her dearly.

Even as a child, I never permitted myself to grieve. I knew I could keep the pain at bay only if I stayed busy. So, the everyday routines that began to feel oppressive before now keep my mind occupied. My father-in-law was a different story.

Dad's grief caused him to drink even more, and it was difficult to see him in such a pitiful condition. We no longer took the children to see him because he was drunk most of the time. Not long after Mom's death, he told us he was seeing another woman. We were introduced to his new friend about three months after Dorothy's death. I guess he found his own way to grieve.

Grandma Bennett also suffered. Her face looked old and haggard, and one day, she blurted out, "I wish I had died instead of my daughter!" A mother should never have to bury her child.

She lived with Carl and Dorothy for many years but didn't feel right about staying alone with her son-in-law. Besides, she needed to be cared for now that she was eighty-six. Her two sons and Dallas and I agreed to move her to a private residence. Within a few months, Grandma Bennett felt like it was her home. After her shop was auctioned off, the final chapter of her life was closed.

Now that his mother was gone, Dallas took the brunt of caring for both his siblings. Susan suffered from bipolar disorder and had trouble coping and making decisions. She called him at the office during the day or sometimes at home long after we had gone to sleep.

These added family pressures were affecting my marriage.

When I needed some help or support from Dallas, I felt ignored. I knew something had to change. It was too bad that I wasn't familiar with all the social service agencies that could have helped; perhaps I wouldn't have felt so helpless or alone.

Even the members of our church failed to offer moral support, even though I knew most of them were aware of our family troubles. I was too embarrassed to talk about my problems with the few close friends I had. Besides, I was not a person who easily shared her feelings.

I was miserable. One weekend, I sat down with Dallas and gave him an ultimatum. I wanted to go back east where my cousin lived. I would take the children, find an apartment, and start a new life. He needed to decide whether it was more important for him to stay in St. Louis or go with us. I never realized my husband wasn't happy about his family's situation either. He had been thinking the same thing, so it didn't take him long to decide.

Looking back, my usual pattern of behavior kicked in: if things didn't work out, I'd just pick up and move. I had done that all my life, but in this particular case, neither Dallas nor I could come up with a better solution.

It wasn't easy for him, but I needed a husband, and our children needed a father. The time was ripe to leave; the family was as stable as they were ever going to be. Dallas requested a transfer, and after living in St. Louis for three and a half years, we were on our way to Minneapolis, Minnesota.

The year was 1972. We found a home in Edina, a beautiful suburb of Minneapolis. It fit our criteria nicely: our main concern was to live in an area with a good school system for our children, and Dallas's office should be close by. Since he traveled a great deal, we wanted the airport to be a reasonable distance from the house. Moving from place to place became my second nature, so I adjusted quickly and easily. As soon as I was settled in, I had to find new ways to stay busy. I didn't know how to sit still and do nothing.

First, we joined a Methodist church, and I offered to help with some of their projects. I also helped out a neighbor who recently lost her husband. I went to nursing homes and visited shut-ins. I liked being busy.

Dallas's job became more demanding as time went by. I had to cut back on volunteering my time to others, although I stayed busy with taking care of our children, maintaining the yard, and keeping the house in apple-pie order.

So, why did I still have bouts of loneliness?

I continued to take my Valium at night and found my restful sleep that way. I would find out soon enough that the medicine was only masking some deeper issues that I needed to address.

During a routine dental checkup, the dentist told me that my teeth were in bad shape. I needed several root canals and some teeth extracted. During Carl's pregnancy, I didn't take calcium supplements and still hated to drink milk. As a result, my teeth became weak. For months, I went to the dentist, but I couldn't get rid of the terrible discomfort in my gums. I refused to give in to the pain, so I threw myself into keeping busy with my household duties. Surprisingly, playing tennis also diverted my focus. Once or twice a week, I took out my frustration by smashing tennis balls.

These distractions worked for a while, but my jaw pain was still there. The dentist was at a loss; he referred me to the Mayo Clinic in Rochester, Minnesota. My husband and I drove to the clinic on a dreary, drizzly day. Alone with our thoughts, we didn't talk a lot, but I fervently hoped for a cure. After many tests, the doctors concluded that I had neuropathy for which there was no medical cure. Two options were proposed: I could enter a chronic pain hospital where patients were treated with Valium and other narcotics, or I could try a fairly new but successful chronic pain program started by Dr. Loran Pilling, a psychiatrist.

On the way back home, Dallas voiced his opinion. "This is preposterous; of all the people I know, no one is saner than you! You're so strong. You're the survivor, the fixer—you need a psychiatrist?"

Then he lapsed into silence. Soft music drifted from the radio, and the soothing sound calmed him. A little later, I turned off the radio so Dallas could hear me clearly when I reassured him that I could handle everything. I'd still be a good wife and mother and still keep up with my tennis and volunteer work.

Dallas sighed heavily. Psychiatry was a mystery to him; most people did not accept the concept either. He wasn't convinced by a long shot that it would help me.

———❦———

For several months, I was able to handle the pain in my jaw. The pain that developed in my back, however, turned from a dull ache to persistent agony. I couldn't function anymore, and my husband and friends encouraged me to see an orthopedist.

My tennis companion, Mary Hartwig, and I played every Wednesday, and I knew her husband, John, was an orthopedist. I decided to make an appointment with him.

During the first meeting, Dr. Hartwig made me feel comfortable. He was a tall and slender man. His cheekbones stood out, and his blue eyes spoke kindness. I thought his wavy gray hair was distinctive and dashing. We chatted briefly, and I mentioned that I was from Germany.

"But I was Gerda Hartwich back then."

"Really?" he said. "We could be distant relatives, you know." He explained that Americans could not pronounce the "ch" properly, and his relatives had changed it to a "g." Then he got serious. "So why are you here?"

I recapped the visit to the Mayo Clinic, which was prompted by my chronic jaw pain. "I must be worrying too much," I admitted. "The jaw pain isn't that bad; I can handle that. It's my back that's really causing me a lot of pain."

"Let's schedule some tests and see what we can find," Dr. Hartwig said.

Over a period of several months, I had a myelogram, discograms, a soft body brace, and a hard brace, but nothing helped. I was so depressed, and I felt hopeless.

Occasionally, I turned to my husband for companionship. I thought if I could talk to him about all the hardships I experienced during and after the war, I would feel better. Dallas wasn't much of a conversationalist, and his silence often made me sad. It's not that he didn't care; he just didn't know how to help. Then my tears would flow. The next day, he would buy me flowers or a box of candy. The gesture was touching, and his effort usually chased the blues away… at least until the next time.

I never knew when the next bout of depression would hit. Sometimes, it happened when I least expected it. For instance, one night, as I soaked in a warm bubble bath, a crushing sadness overwhelmed me. I thought about how much responsibility my husband had to shoulder since my back trouble started. After working all day, he had to come home and take care of the children. I couldn't even stand long enough to cook a meal, so Dallas had to bring home take-out food almost every night.

I realized how lucky Kim and Carl were to have a father who was willing to take on the additional role of being a mother. He read to them every night and wasn't too tired to play games with them. Who would actually miss me if I weren't around? I couldn't think of a single person other than Dallas. I even contemplated suicide.

I knew I had to rid myself of this self-pity before it destroyed me. I needed to be strong for the children. Maybe I should reconsider the referral to Dr. Pilling's clinic.

I knew a little bit about the man: Pilling had received his medical training at the Mayo Clinic. He first studied internal medicine, then became a psychiatrist, and founded his own clinic. Before I could talk myself out of it, I called his office and made an appointment.

I had one week to get ready. I was so desperate that I didn't care what my neighbors or church friends might say behind my back. Dallas was still not convinced that I had made the right choice, but he was willing to let me try.

I was determined to change the course of my life. Again!

CHAPTER 7

SETTLING INTO THE CLINIC

Our days at the clinic were hectic. First, we had breakfast in the cafeteria, followed by floor exercises, relaxation technique sessions, and water aerobics. Then came lunch. We all needed to replenish our energy because the afternoons were just as busy. First, occupational therapy was followed by group and individual therapy. In addition, I had individual sessions with Dr. Pilling once a week.

After dinner, we often listened to an evening lecture, and family and friends were encouraged to attend. Dallas chose to join me, but I think my friends were too scared to come. Dr. Pilling stressed the importance of these lectures to the visitors: "Your loved ones are learning new ways to express their needs and emotions. You should support them."

One of the topics for the evening lecture was about alcohol and drug abuse. Dr. Pilling's opinion was that he believed some drugs could hinder our mental stability.

I had been taking Valium for ten years. Since 1968, I had been taking a pill every night so I could sleep. The doctor who prescribed it said it would do me good, which was true. However, to benefit from all the advice I was getting at the clinic, I knew I had to confess about my nightly Valium pill to Dr. Pilling.

He promptly recommended that I should wean myself off of this narcotic drug. I wanted to get better fast, so I quit cold turkey. Despite some withdrawal symptoms, I didn't relapse. I trusted Dr. Pilling's advice that I'd be better off without this medication.

Of course, once I quit, sleeping became more difficult than ever, and if I dozed off, I usually woke up overwhelmed with emotions. Sometimes, I didn't know whether to dissolve into a pool of tears or to beat up my pillow. I was on an emotional roller coaster and didn't know how to get off.

After a few days, I considered leaving the clinic. The interaction with other patients and therapists—including Dr. Pilling—was so intense that I felt more confused.

I needed a good sounding board. In desperation, I called my dear friend Janice Dobies, who had a PhD in psychology. Her demure appearance was deceptive—she could deliver straight talk when it was needed. I felt proud and honored to have her as my friend and took her advice to heart.

"Gerda, let me tell you something," she said. "You're in the right place. Maybe things don't make much sense yet, but give it a few more days, and you'll understand how this program works.

"Let me give you an analogy," she continued. "Imagine an onion with many layers. As we mature, more layers are added. If someone doesn't get the proper nurturing care, and your pain and feelings haven't been expressed, the layers build up. By the time you're an adult, you've formed a thick, hard skin like the outside of an onion. As we continue to live, those outer layers protect us; even sensitive emotions can't pierce through that tough exterior. Neither the love of God nor any love and tenderness can penetrate."

I was still too distraught to think clearly, but she convinced me to stay and give the clinic a second chance. She also promised to talk to me again. I trusted her enough to take her advice, and I stayed.

After a couple more days of eye-opening therapy, I noticed I was losing my balance. I had to hold on to the railings to steady myself as I walked through the halls, and this really frightened me.

When I mentioned my dizziness to Dr. Pilling, he kindly reassured me by explaining how the body behaves in strange ways.

"Remember, Gerda, you have suppressed and stored your emotions for many years, and slowly, we are putting you in touch with them again." He acknowledged my concern about my physical imbalance, but he wasn't a bit surprised by it. "Stay with the program. If you had learned early in life how important it was to express your emotions, you wouldn't have to go through this." He continued to explain that if we don't use our emotions regularly, it's like letting any of our limbs go idle. They atrophy, and the body no longer functions as a whole.

The professional staff repeated often, "You are here to learn the life-saving skills that will heal you; you just have to trust us that it's going to work."

I tried to take comfort in their mantra, but in reality, I felt like a zombie, more dead than alive. If anybody had told me I was stupid and worthless and should kill myself, I think I might have done it at the time.

Like an obedient child, I followed the rules and participated in every activity as required. The number-one rule, and a surprising one, was: Don't talk about your pain. All of us were here because our lives had been turned upside down and shaken apart by chronic pain—and we weren't supposed to talk about it? What a stupid rule!

During one of the lectures, the reason became clear: if you

continually talked about pain, the brain intensified it. Okay, maybe not a stupid rule.

We all hated Thursdays. That's when Dr. Pilling and the staff put us in the hot seat during group sessions. In front of the whole group, all of the staff members would tell Dr. Pilling what they observed about each patient and what they had to learn. All the patients squirmed under such close scrutiny.

Denny, my personal therapist, announced one Thursday, "Gerda is a hard worker and wants to do what's best, but she needs to lower her expectations of herself and others." He proceeded to give some examples. "Gerda thinks she has to do everything perfectly. If she can't, she gets frustrated and gives up. She also needs to fix other people's problems."

The first time I heard those insulting words, they stung like a bee, and I seethed with anger inside. I felt like my inadequacies were paraded around for all to see and criticize. I was glad when we were finally released from the hot seat session. Although it was difficult for me to hear these character assessments, I took them seriously enough to try to fix them as soon as I could.

After dinner that night, I called the children to see how Uncle Gilbert was coping with his new responsibilities. Gilbert was kind enough to fill in as "mom" while I was at the clinic. They all sounded good, and Kim told me dinner was almost on the table. In a motherly-sounding tone, she said, "Oh, don't worry, Mom. We're fine, and I told Uncle Gilbert he could set the table."

Dallas stopped by after work, and I had the feeling that he could see all my internal sorrow on my face. I knew that this was hard for him, too. He gave me a reassuring smile despite his worried look. When he left, he gave me a big hug and said, "Hang in there, my sweet Gerda. I love you."

It was such an emotionally charged day for me. I crawled into bed, my mind filled with doubt and confusion. It was earlier than my usual bedtime, and my mind was not ready for sleep. My emotions were running rampant through my brain. All of a sudden, I had the urge to get out of bed and pray.

Tante Erna's philosophy was this: "God only listens to us when we are on our knees."

Up until then, I rejected that idea—my stubbornness would not allow me to kneel. I had thought that God listened to us whether we were lying down or standing up.

But now I was kneeling on that cold linoleum. "Where are you, Jesus? I need you," I began.

I thanked Him for carrying me through many hard times in Germany. "You protected me from the air raids; you were with me when I had diphtheria. Even though I was cold and hungry, you didn't let me perish. When I was a teenager, I could have strayed from a righteous life, but I didn't. I survived my mother's death and my father's physical and emotional abuse, and I even left my country and my siblings behind. Oh, God, where are you?"

"You brought me to this wonderful country. You gave me a loving husband and two beautiful children. Those two kids mean more to me than my life. They are my family, and I thank you for them. Please, God, do not forsake me. Have mercy on me and show me the way. I am totally helpless, and I need you. Change me and make me whole." I ended my fervent prayer with, "Thank you, God. I know that you hear my cry. Amen." My Tante Erna's favorite amen—she would be proud of me!

I dragged my tired and tense body back to bed. As I lay on my back with my hands still folded in prayer, every bone and muscle in my body felt like Jell-O. A sense of peace filled my soul after the fervent plea I just uttered. This relaxed sensation lasted about twenty seconds, but I had never felt better. My last thought before I fell asleep was that some infinite power had created me and was watching over my actions and my thoughts.

When I awoke, I pushed back the covers, stood up, and walked to the mirror. I looked at my face—peering back at me was a stranger who looked like she was on the verge of death. At that moment, a fierce resolve came over me, and with newfound determination, I vowed, "You will get better, not only for yourself, but for Dallas, Kim, and Carl, too."

With a new, single-minded purpose, I pulled a bright blue sweater out of my drawer, put on a little lipstick, and was quite pleased with these minor improvements. My step was springier when I entered the cafeteria for breakfast, and I managed a pleasant smile when greeting my fellow patients.

Nancy, my neighbor-patient, noticed the change right away. "You look perky this morning, Gerda. You must have slept well."

It felt so wonderful to hear her positive remark.

With renewed energy, I went to the next group meeting. The discussion was about anger, and it seemed like everyone had an opinion on the subject. Denny's eyes scanned the group and then settled on me.

"Gerda, how do you handle anger?" he asked.

With a brash tone, I announced that Dallas and I never went to bed angry. The whole group laughed out loud.

"It's no wonder you're here with chronic pain," someone said. I wanted to run from the room; I felt humiliated and stupid. Denny jotted down something in his notebook, and I

143

figured this topic would be included in our next meeting.

As painful as the group sessions were, every day, I noticed that my mind opened a little more. We started talking about our relationships, not only with our spouses but with in-laws, friends, neighbors, and co-workers. We learned that stress is the biggest impairment to our health and that whether the burden is physical or mental, it has the same effect.

Dr. Pilling gave us an example. He said that people who do well at mentally handling their diabetes, cancer, or any other ailment usually see their illness stabilize. This notion really made an impression on me, especially when he said, "You'd be surprised by how many people die from the fear of death itself." Dr. Pilling stressed that how we communicate and handle our daily lives determines our health. What an interesting concept!

One of my assignments was dealing with Marie, a slender, petite woman with perfect white teeth who lived across the street from me in Edina. Despite a few wrinkles and some silver threads beginning to show in her dark hair, she was an attractive woman. Marie and her husband John didn't have children, but they were the proud "parents" of Muffy, an adorable white poodle. They took their obsession further by celebrating Mother's Day and Father's Day with Muffy substituting as their child.

Almost every morning, after the children went to school, Marie came to our house unannounced. This went on for a long time, and I started to begrudge these impositions, but I didn't know how to stop it. I felt it was my Christian duty to welcome her into my home. She often said, "Gerda, it's so nice that you spend time with me every morning." Sometimes, she'd even add wistfully, "After our visit, I know I can make it through the rest of the day."

I felt guilty about sending her away or not answering the door when she knew darn well I was home.

This became a big topic of discussion at the clinic. The therapists role-played with me, trying to teach me how to say no to her. Dr.

Pilling also asked me a few questions to try to understand my obligatory feelings toward Marie.

"Can she not drive?" he asked. "Does she not have a car?" "Is she handicapped in some way?" "Is she blind?"

The answer was always no.

"Then why on earth do you feel obligated to babysit her? It appears to me that she's taking advantage of you."

Like so many things at the clinic, this revelation was difficult for me to hear and harder for me to act on.

"Let me ask you this," continued Dr. Pilling. "Do you like her?" "Yes," I replied, "but when she's around, I feel I'm losing control of my time."

"Do you want to change that?"

I didn't have to think that one over for too long. I said, "Yes, but I need help to handle the situation kindly and gently." So we worked on that.

Ellen was another good friend of mine. She and her husband lived in the neighborhood in a beautiful home bordering a small lake. The first time I entered the house, my eyes were drawn to the pretty willow tree framed by a bay window.

Ellen was an attractive woman with a petite figure and dark, curly hair. Her twinkling eyes and athletic movements spoke of her robust health. But she and her husband Jim really loved their martinis. In fact, Jim called ahead before he left the office so the freshly made cocktails were ready the instant he walked through the door.

Ellen had a fondness for Kim and Carl. Her childless status prompted several dinner invitations, especially when Dallas was away on business.

"Bring the children," she'd coax. "Everything is ready. I'm sure you don't feel like cooking when your husband is out of town."

Often, I'd politely answer that I appreciated the offer but wanted to stay home that night. She was relentless, however; after insisting that we be their guests, I always gave in.

Denny gently reminded me, "Gerda, you have a hard time saying no to people, don't you?" I had to admit he was right—I was afraid to say no.

"Why is that?" he asked.

"I don't know," I said, wringing my hands.

Denny prodded further. "Is it because you don't want to feel abandoned?"

I nodded in agreement. Denny scribbled in his notebook, and I felt like a child who got caught stealing.

Slowly, the relationship between the body and the mind became clearer. These two factions were connected, and I started to realize how devastating mental stress was to my physical health.

———

There was so much information being thrown at me in a

group session one day that I threw up my hands and stood up. "I need a break, Denny!"

"I certainly understand," he assured me. "I've been there myself— it's called 'fried brain.'" He grinned. "By the way, Gerda, did I tell you we're planning to go to the movies for Fun Night?"

I wasn't too thrilled. Going to the movies wasn't going to help me get well. Besides, I would rather go with Dallas or my friends.

"Look at it this way," Denny said, addressing the whole group. "When you have a lot of stressful days together, families tend to get burned out. Some family members get stuck in this mode and get depressed; others experience chronic pain. What I'm doing is introducing some fun time to break the cycle, that's all." He shrugged his shoulders. "By the way, there's a party at the end of the program, so you might as well get used to the idea. Just hang loose and enjoy the ride!"

I decided I liked the movie just fine. And I had fun.

Friday came. It was the end of my first week, and I was glad the group session went well. At least it paved the way for an enjoyable weekend. I was looking forward to seeing my family, as were the other patients—except one: Helen.

Helen, who had been quiet most of the time, finally spoke up. "Dr. Pilling, I'm tired of hearing how wonderful our weekend is going to be. Let me tell you something: when I go home, I follow the instructions you've pounded in my head. I tell my husband and kids that I'm not their maid, and I'm tired of waiting on them hand and foot," she said, ticking off the items on her fingers. "Then I tell them they all have to help out, like normal families do." Helen turned up her palms. "They all listen and then disappear. I feel lousy and do all the work myself. I feel like I'm talking to a wall."

"Helen, what do you expect?" asked Dr. Pilling. "Your family has used you like a doormat for a while. It takes time, patience, and a lot of repetition before you see any changes. But it has to start with you. We are going to teach you new ways of thinking and give you new tools that eventually will bring results."

He continued by saying, "You have to set the stage and let everyone know that you want their full attention, and they can't leave the room until you're finished talking. Have your plan all worked out—who will do what chore, and when will you expect it done? If you don't have an agenda, it's like an orchestra trying to play without a conductor. The theory about 'getting it off your chest to make you feel better' is no longer valid. What we are looking for is a response to what we say. Make eye contact, and don't let them get away without a response. Try it. I think it will work for you if you put it into practice, not once but over and over again."

I listened intently to Dr. Pilling's philosophy. The wheels spun my head, and I filed it away for future reference. I might need to apply this strategy at home, as well as in other situations where I tend to be too quick to say yes without thinking the matter through.

But now I was anxious to get home so I could hug my children. As I stood by the window waiting for Dallas to pick me up, a thousand thoughts flashed through my head. I learned so much in the past seven days, but I was still confused. Mostly, I challenged my quick decision to leave Germany. If I had stayed, how would my life have turned out? Would I have had a loving, supportive family there? Had the war affected my mental health? Was I too German to ever fit in America? I even questioned my marriage to Dallas, and that truly scared me the most.

The floodgates of my mind were opened, and the water was dragging me downstream to an uncertain destination. Denny saw my distress, and he came over and put his hand on my shoulder. He reminded me that I was doing a lot of hard work.

"It will get better," he assured me.

Dallas arrived and gave me a friendly hello and a hug. "Let's go home," he said. The after-work rush-hour traffic was heavy. When the cars came to a standstill, Dallas and I stared out the window, listening to his favorite classical music station on the radio. I wanted to tell him about my first week at the clinic but was too meek to express my wishes.

I've got to work on not being so submissive, I vowed to myself. I'm sure Denny or Dr. Pilling could give me advice but in the meantime,

I just sat there feeling sad that Dallas preferred to listen to the radio instead of me.

Maybe we weren't the happy couple I once thought we were. Just because we didn't quarrel didn't mean we had a blissful marriage. Dallas and I never argued because our conversations rarely scratched the surface of our true feelings. We lived to work and worked to live, so our conversations revolved around the practical things in life: household duties, work responsibilities, and raising children. This was going to have to change.

With that resolution firmly entrenched in my brain, I became more impatient to see the children as we got closer to home. As soon as they heard the car, Kim and Carl burst through the front door, followed by Duchess, our English Springer. Kids were running, the dog was jumping, and in all the commotion, I almost got knocked over. I was so happy to be home.

"Oh, I missed you!" I gathered up Kim and Carl in my arms, drawing them close. "I could just eat you up!" I gave them lots of kisses.

They gleefully shouted out a hundred things all at once. I couldn't understand a thing they said, so I just listened, a big smile plastered across my face. I noticed how frazzled Uncle Gilbert looked, and his shoulders visibly relaxed when I stepped into the house.

Weekends like this came and went. I continued taking part in the clinic's weekly regimen, but my sleepless nights still haunted me. Most evenings, I lay on my back, paralyzed with doubt about getting better. Sometimes, I dreamed that a wolf was chasing me. Dr. Pilling assured me this was all part of the healing process, so I trusted him implicitly.

I had a sore throat one morning and pleaded to stay in bed. Dr. Pilling examined me and said, "You're fine. Remember that physical symptoms are common when you're dealing with emotions." After a while, I committed myself to following his advice until the day I was deemed well enough to go home. I felt like a butterfly being released from a box; it was time for me to exercise my wings.

The day I was discharged, my head was crammed with all the lessons I'd learned at the clinic. I was apprehensive about the challenges I still faced ahead. Denny gave me a big hug, and with a broad smile, he said, "You're a great lady, and I hope to see you again."

"Not me," I joked. "I need to go home and recuperate from your wounds."

It felt good to tease him a little. Denny was tough on me

sometimes, but I knew how gentle and compassionate he was. He did it for my own good. Before Dallas came to pick me up, Denny gave me a last piece of advice.

"Remember what I've taught you: express what you're feeling. That's part of the healing process." He warned me, "You're too special a person; don't allow others to take advantage of you. Gerda, you're a young, attractive woman who's kind and giving."

Every one of those words made an imprint on my heart. From now on, I wouldn't be so eager to put my happiness behind everyone else's, and the first step was my marriage.

I already made up my mind that Dallas and I needed counseling. In one of my sessions with Dr. Pilling, I inquired about a good marriage counselor. From his pocket, he pulled out Dr. William Hanley's business card. I figured Dr. Pilling had many such requests from his patients since he kept the cards within easy reach.

I also decided to take part in an outpatient lecture program. I would be able to take refresher courses to retain what I learned, and I could join a support group if I needed it.

When I arrived home, I felt different than when I left: stronger and more focused. My husband made it clear he was glad I was home, although being a man of few words, he didn't say so. Of course, I was eager to resume taking care of the kids and the house. I cut back on my volunteer work and practiced what I had learned at the clinic.

Now that I was home, I had to deal with Marie, the pesky neighbor across the street. I thought about Denny's advice: Don't let people take advantage of you.

I called her on the telephone. "I don't feel well this morning, and it would be better if we didn't visit. I hope that's

151

all right with you." She took it well, and I was glad I had taken that first step.

In the days that followed, she never came over again or even called to ask how I was. It occurred to me that she might have been afraid to talk with someone who had mental health issues. In the early '70s, many people were leery when they heard the word "psychiatrist."

Although I was happy to be rid of my neighbor's daily visits, I felt alone. Many of my friends and neighbors had gone back to work. Dallas became consumed with his demanding job, and I needed to release everything swirling around my head and heart. I felt guilty about my anger because my husband was such a hardworking man.

How fortuitous to find something to fill the void. The radio became my daily companion. Dr. Charles Swindoll, a preacher from California, hosted a program that I listened to with keen interest. Getting closer to God was still a priority with me. As I listened to the preacher, the message sank deeper into my soul. His sermons sounded like they were tailor-made for me. I asked God to tell me what I should do.

"You gave me a good husband. Please, God, help me learn to love him again."

My prayer was answered. I started to feel more contented about my life after I did my prescribed exercises and relaxation techniques. Listening to the radio programs helped, too. I regained my strength and was able to lighten Dallas's weekend chores to make it easier for him. We started going back to Richfield United Methodist Church, where we had been members before. We put the children in Sunday school classes, and I made an effort to find my way within the congregation.

I wasn't prepared for another setback. One day, one of the

church ladies came up to me and whispered in my ear, "Are you still going to that place?" I was shocked and humiliated.

I remember that during one of my outpatient sessions, a health worker said that ignorance and a lack of sensitivity are quite common when dealing with laypeople. But that warning didn't protect me from the hurt and sadness.

I took another approach. If I made a connection with the minister, perhaps the church would become a more comfortable place. I visited him with the express purpose of volunteering my time to work in the office. It was only half a day per week, but he appreciated the offer, and we shook off it.

Odd, I thought, walking back to the car; why didn't he ask me how I was doing?

I worked in the office for several weeks, and no one, including the minister, offered me a cup of coffee or struck up a conversation with me. I decided to leave this cold environment, so I quit. I was convinced that listening to Dr. Swindoll on the radio was more beneficial than going to church. I suppose that some ministers feel awkward talking to a person with a mental health condition.

Dr. James Dobson, a child psychologist who was also on the radio worldwide, had a program called Focus on the Family. He wrote numerous books about families and faith. I started listening to his show, too, and was thankful both programs were being broadcast. They helped me grow in my spiritual journey, and I learned a lot about communication and how to raise kids.

I always recognized that our kids were lucky to have a father who played games with them and tucked them in with a bedtime story. As a stay-at-home mother, I usually doled out the discipline and guidance. But after learning more about myself, I found it easier to have fun with the kids when Dallas was away on business trips.

We used to turn up the music and dance with abandon. Since Dallas grew up listening to classical music, he didn't appreciate the kids' current songs. After he and I started going to counseling, I made him a deal: for every half hour of classical music we listened to, the kids were allowed to play a half hour of rock and roll.

I wanted to go back to church, but not Richfield. I learned the hard way that I wasn't wanted there. The Congregational Church in Edina had a strong reputation for being active, friendly, and supportive, plus our children had friends who attended there. Dallas and the kids were fine with the decision to make this church our new home, which remained for as long as we lived there.

CHAPTER 8
THOSE COLD BLUE EYES-
SEVENTEEN YEARS LATER

My debilitating backache subsided, and I continued my outpatient program at the clinic. How amazing to be free of the pain. Although I made great strides with therapy, my emotions still surged up and down.

During one of the outpatient sessions, Dr. Pilling noticed how I distanced myself from everyone by sitting in the corner. I didn't make eye contact with anyone, nor did I engage in idle talk with anybody. He came over and sat next to me.

"How is Gerda doing?" he asked, gently taking my hand in his. Tears spilled down my face. "Well, Dr. Pilling, I think I might be homesick." I gave him a tight smile. "Did you know I left my entire family seventeen years ago and haven't seen them since?"

Gently, he said, "I was wondering how long it would take you to revisit all the unfinished business you left behind." He patted my hand. "You know, Gerda, our society would be a lot healthier if everyone learned how to express and process their emotions." With a little laugh, he added, "Tying up the loose ends wouldn't hurt either."

"My life is full of loose ends," I admitted.

"I can see," he said. "You know, I've had people in my office who start crying immediately after I ask them why they're upset.

Then they tell me their mother or husband or whoever has died, and they haven't cried since it happened. Stored-up

155

feelings can cause a lot of pain emotionally and physically, but I have a suspicion you understand this already."

"Yes, and that's why I have to go. I've put it off long enough." I put on a brave face, but my conviction sounded weak. I had been back to Germany several times since leaving in 1961, but never to face the pain of my past.

"I have every faith that you will do fine, but I sense your doubt." I nodded. "I'm afraid that I'm not strong enough," I admitted, amazed by how well this man could read my thoughts.

"I certainly don't doubt your strength." He looked me in the eye. "You'll be fine."

"Can I ask a favor? Would you mind giving me your office and home phone number—in case I get sick?" I asked. I didn't want to get into a German hospital under any circumstances. Traumatic childhood memories of doctors and hospitals still haunted me. "I'm also having trouble with bouts of laughing and crying. That scares me, too."

"Well, you've been dredging up a lot of emotional events from your past. It usually stirs up big waves; when things settle down, the waves get smaller," he reassured me.

I was hesitant to ask him if he could prescribe me a few Valium tablets, just in case I got too exhausted and couldn't sleep. I reminded him that he took me off them a few weeks ago.

"I don't think that'll be a problem at all," he said. "Besides, I know you won't abuse them."

After Dr. Pilling boosted my confidence, I made up my mind to go. The year was 1978, and at the age of forty, I booked a flight to Germany, determined to put my ghosts to rest. But I had to do it alone.

Dallas and the children would stay home. He made arrangements to work half days so he could watch Kim and Carl after school. All I had to do now was trust my gut instincts that I was doing the right thing.

A violent rainstorm swept through Minneapolis the morning of my flight, and it threatened to delay my trip. Thankfully, my plane took off on schedule. I was determined to confront my father and any other unpleasant memories that lingered in the place where I grew up.

The vast expanse of ocean glided underneath me as I quieted my jumpy nerves.

I arrived in Frankfurt early in the morning. Jet lag pulled at my weary bones as I made my way through the airport. I made a valiant effort to muster up some excitement, but putting one foot in front of the other was all I could manage.

Soon, I was on a northbound train, barely able to keep my eyes open while the landscape sped by. It took a moment to realize how beautiful the scenery was. Gone were the ruins and devastation of war; in their stead were brightly painted houses and beautiful flower gardens and majestic trees waving in the wind. I wanted to stop the train and jump out to kiss the earth!

I glanced around, hoping someone would share my joy, but the people around me were used to the stunning sights.

As the train rattled on, I became fascinated with the rhythm of the wheels. The clattering pattern halted once in a while when people got either on or off. I tried to close my eyes and get some rest, but I was too keyed up to sleep despite being awake for eighteen hours. I mulled over my feelings about seeing my siblings again.

As I got closer to Wilhelmshaven, I felt my pulse rise. It wouldn't be long before Ilse and her husband Heinz would greet me at the station. To my amazement, I never felt any back pain as I wrestled my suitcase from the overhead compartment. Eagerly, I stood by the door, ready to jump out as soon as the train stopped.

I recognized Ilse right away. Although she had gained a few pounds, I kept reminding myself how many years had passed since we last saw each other. One thing didn't change: her blond hair was still short and curly.

Our eyes welled up with tears as we flew into each other's arms and hugged for a long time. When we finally broke the embrace, Heinz and I shook hands vigorously. He was tall and slender and—as I learned later—had a green thumb.

Their house was spacious and well-appointed. I eyed the plush couch and wished I could take a nap. But Heinz wanted to show off his backyard. Neat flowerbeds bloomed on the perimeter of the lush lawn. Not a blade of grass seemed out of place. Heinz was especially proud of his thriving vegetable garden and blossoming fruit trees. My eyes absorbed the abundance of color splashed all around, and I looked forward to spending some time out here.

Now that I had toured their beautiful home, they wanted to catch up with my family in America. I showed them pictures of my husband, the kids, and our house. The rest of the day was filled with lots of chatter and laughter as we reconnected our roots.

That night, my niece, Angelika, grabbed my hand and showed me her lovely room. I was touched when she insisted I stay there, and I thanked her profusely. I slipped under the down comforter and thanked God for my safe trip.

Sleep evaded me for a long time. I contemplated taking one of the Valiums I had tucked in my suitcase, but I resisted. My head reeled with the one visit I dreaded the most: my father. The image of his angry blue eyes pierced my soul, and my old insecurities surfaced.

Dr. Pilling had reassured me many times that I would feel better after I faced my father, but I didn't share his confidence at the moment.

I'll think about it tomorrow, I told myself as I rolled over and closed my eyes.

I woke in a dark room, and it took me a few seconds to orient myself. When I looked at my watch, I jumped out of bed. I could hardly believe it was almost ten o'clock!

Ilse was sitting at the breakfast table when I ambled into the small kitchen.

"Hey, sleepyhead, glad you finally woke up," she teased. "I thought I'd let you sleep since you'd been up for so long."

I sat down at the table and admired the cozy room. Everything was spic and span. On the windowsill, a parakeet chirped in his cage. "Meet Peter," Ilse said, pointing to the bird. "He doesn't have a pretty voice, but he sure tries hard." Then she explained that because her kids were rarely around, the noisy bird filled the emptiness.

I knew how she felt.

The table was set with a typical German breakfast: fresh-baked rolls with butter and a variety of cold cuts and cheeses. Of course, a wide selection of jams and preserves were placed in the middle of the table. Northern Germans usually drink tea, but since Ilse knew I liked coffee, she had made it especially for me. I thought the effort was sweet. The radio played familiar German tunes in the background as we cradled the hot cups in our hands. Inhaling the aroma of freshly brewed coffee, I wished we lived closer so we could enjoy these moments more often.

"When are you going to visit our father?" she asked, shattering the idyllic moment.

"Never!" I was quick to reply, but we knew it was a lie. "Let's not spoil a good meal," I reasoned. "I know I have to see him … I just don't want to rush it."

"I know how you feel," she replied. "I don't see him very much, and that's how I like it."

Suddenly, I had the urge to get the burden out of the way. Now. This instant.

I blurted out, "Let's call the bastard!"

Ilse stared at me, her mouth wide open. We rarely called him "father," but "bastard" was pretty extreme. More often, we referred to him as *der Alte*, the old man. Tante Erna scolded us at times. "You should show him some respect!" But she didn't know how cruel he was, and she tended not to believe us.

"Give me his phone number," I said boldly. "I'm going to call him right now." When he picked up, however, the bluster in my voice was gone. "Hello, this is Gerda," I squeaked.

"So, my long-lost daughter is here. When are you coming over?" I told him Ilse and I could be there within the hour.

"You can have coffee with Dora and me," he said. Click— that was the end of our conversation.

As we drove through town, I was amazed by the restoration of the buildings. I hardly recognized the area, and it was a reminder of how long I had been gone. If Ilse hadn't been driving, I would have missed the turn to Allmersstrasse in Neuengroden, where we lived for more than ten years.

When we pulled up to our old apartment, my stomach churned. After climbing up to the second floor, I froze when I stood in front of the door. Ilse took the initiative and rang the bell.

"*Gruess Dich*, Greetings," Dora said, opening the door. My father stood behind his wife of nineteen years, and I stretched out my hand to him. I preferred a strong handshake instead of an awkward hug.

We sat in the living room, and I brought out my photos to pass around. After the pictures were back in my purse, I sat quietly until I was asked a question. The visit turned out to be rather bland, and I was surprised by how calm I felt.

In between bits of conversation, I looked around the room, trying to remember what it looked like when my mother lived there. I don't remember the rooms being so small, although I liked the new floors that had been installed. Coffee and cake were served on their good china.

Why I had fretted about this moment was beyond me. Now that I was here, sitting on the soft green furniture, I wasn't anxious at all. I might even try to forgive him for being a rotten father. After I convinced myself that he could no longer hurt me, that he was no longer in charge of me, I felt like a thousand pounds had been lifted from my shoulders. When I said goodbye, it wasn't surprising that he didn't invite me to come again. Ilse didn't invite him over to her house either.

As I was lying in bed that night, I thought of all the pain and suffering I had endured in my life, and I couldn't hold back the tears anymore. I cried until I got rid of the deep sorrow within me. Eventually, I fell asleep.

Over the next few days, Ilse and I found ways to relax by shopping and eating out for lunch together. I also saw our siblings and their families when Ilse invited them for dinner one evening. When it was time to leave Wilhelmshaven, Ilse drove me to the train station, where we said our teary goodbyes. I took the train to Hagen and had a wonderful visit with Tante Erna for a day or two before continuing on to Frankfort for my flight home.

I spent about a week in Germany, and my emotions were raw most of that time. I remember how angry I got when my brother-in-law criticized the United States. I wasn't born in America, but I now consider it my home. My husband and the kids were so far away, and I missed them dearly. I also missed my friends and neighbors.

When the day arrived for me to return to Minneapolis, I was glad to be going home.

CHAPTER 9

INSIDE THE PRESSURE COOKER

I had been home from Germany for about a week. I continued listening to the preachers on the radio because they gave me great comfort. However, my prayer activities needed expanding, so I was delighted to attend a bible study group at the home of a Baptist friend, Gloria.

Shortly after that, I volunteered to host the bible study at my house, and I looked forward to it. On the day the group was scheduled to meet, I recall how I opened the windows to let the fresh June breezes permeate the house. Outside, the birds sang; inside, my heart felt light. It was one of those perfect moments when I was grateful for all the beautiful things God had created.

The doorbell rang—they were here. Soon, all five of us members were engrossed with the lesson. A little later, I noticed how pushy Gloria was, especially when she demanded my time.

"I know what you need, Gerda," Gloria insisted. "You and I ought to have a prayer session and bible reading at least three days a week—maybe even more."

Excuse me, I wanted to say. I suppose I should have been grateful that she wanted to help, but I resented being treated like a child.

Gloria reminded me of my father, and she triggered the control issues I had with him. If I was guilty of overreacting to the situation, it was because I had just returned from Germany.

163

"Gee, I'm sorry, Gloria," I said firmly. "I'm planning to attend a study group at my church, so I won't be able to devote my time to you."

We completed our study and devotion and had our usual cake and coffee afterward. But I felt glad that I had been armed with positive ways to express my feelings and proud that I had used my new skill.

Later that day, I finished a few chores in the house and managed to do a little yard work. While weeding the flower bed, I pondered Gloria's impolite and demanding treatment earlier, and my anger flared up again. Surrounded by the majestic blue spruces and a riot of colorful flowers, I tried to focus on God's beauty like I did this morning.

The peaceful feeling didn't return, and by the time I started thinking about dinner, I had the worst headache ever. I tried an ice pack, but it didn't relieve the pounding in my head. I decided to attend the hospital outpatient program that night. What a godsend that I had this available to me.

When Kim and Carl came home from school, I asked if they would mind getting their own snack. Sitting in front of the TV with cookies and milk, they were quiet until Dallas came home from work. He looked at my face and asked, "What's wrong?"

"My head hurts right on top; it feels like a pressure cooker that's about to explode," I muttered softly. It hurt to talk, but I continued, "I took a Tylenol and used an ice pack, but nothing helped. I'm going to Dr. Pilling's lecture tonight."

Dallas knew it was useless to persuade me to stay home. Excruciating back pain didn't deter me before; I'd take a cab if all else failed.

The drive to the lecture was more difficult than I had

164

anticipated; the rush-hour traffic exacerbated my headache, but I pressed on. Turning into the parking lot, I spotted Dr. Pilling. I ran to catch up and grabbed his sleeve.

"Oh, Dr. Pilling, can you help me? I have a splitting headache!" "I'm sorry to hear that," he said. "You must be stuffing a lot of unresolved issues in there, am I right?"

I had to agree. "When I came back from Germany a week ago, my husband wanted a quick, fifteen-minute report. After that, he never mentioned the trip. I had quite an emotional time there, but he didn't want to talk about it. As far as he was concerned, the subject was closed."

"So, what prevents you from sitting Dallas down and telling him anything you want, no matter how long it takes you?"

"Well, I feel bad because he works so hard. I really don't want to bother him."

Dr. Pilling countered, "Your consideration is admirable, but when will you learn to take care of yourself? Don't you understand that you need to love yourself and care for yourself before you can help anybody else?"

I let that sink in for a moment.

Dr. Pilling invited me to stay for the lecture if I wanted to, but he recommended I go home and take care of my unfinished business. He smiled. "I can almost guarantee that your headache will disappear."

I immediately turned around and headed home.

He makes it sound easy, I thought as I drove back. But I knew he was right. Dallas was used to the old me. The one who kept the house took care of the kids, and did a little volunteer work—the one who always needed to do nice things for everybody.

I guess I was guilty of doing lots of "nice things." For example, one summer, I drove every week to a small town in rural Minnesota that could not afford a German teacher. I did this for two months, traveling almost two hours each way to teach eight separate classes. Starting with kindergarten, each session lasted twenty minutes. The students were eager to learn, and the teacher appreciated my effort, but it was exhausting.

So, if Dallas treated me like a person with no needs of her own, it was because I acted like one.

I spent the rest of the drive home organizing my plan, thanks to another tool Dr. Pilling had given me.

When I arrived home, I was glad the kids were playing outside. I walked into the kitchen and placed my hands on my hips. "What are you doing right now?" I asked.

"I brought some work home," he replied.

"That will have to wait. I need to talk to you. Dr. Pilling sent me home and told me you should listen to me until I finish telling you all about my stressful visit to Germany. He said my feelings are all bottled up. I need to share some of my experiences with you, but you don't seem to have the time for me." I kept my pose. "And he said this is the cause of my headaches."

My husband's face showed his displeasure about Dr. Pilling's assessment. But he had my welfare at heart and suggested we go outside and sit on the porch. We talked for an hour and discovered something wonderful together: sharing can be fun. As the evening turned dark, most of my headache was gone.

I learned a valuable lesson that night: it's important that I don't give in so easily. I needed to exercise determination in order to have my feelings validated.

Along with asserting my needs, I also got better at allowing my emotions to surface. Here's a good example: I'm watching a movie in which children are suffering. I often relate their suffering to my own childhood, but I never allowed myself to weep. Now, if I feel like crying, I do. (To this day, however, I can't watch German war movies.)

As part of my healing process, I came to understand that leaving Germany was the right thing for me to do. I recognized without a doubt that all the conflict within me created my physical pain, and I now had effective strategies for dealing with it. I continued listening to my relaxation tapes, I started playing tennis again, and I exercised when my back hurt. It was about time Gerda took care of Gerda.

Life was good. My husband was awarded trips by IBM in recognition of his performance, so we were able to go on fabulous vacations to Bermuda, Florida, and Hawaii. Frequently, we took the children on camping trips, and our family life continued on a positive note.

Through marriage counseling, I learned that Dallas needed time to think after I asked him a question, and I learned to be quiet until he gave me an answer. Occasionally, his reply took too long. "Are you still thinking, or did you forget the question?" I would ask. We laughed at that one. But I was a good student, and the strategy worked.

Edina was an affluent community in Minnesota, and a fair share of the population had college degrees. I was surrounded by educated friends and acquaintances and thought that perhaps I should enroll in college. Many people encouraged me: Dr. Pilling, the radio preachers Dr. Swindoll and Dr.

Dobson, and the marriage counselors.

I enrolled at the local community college, accumulated some credits, and then transferred to the University of Minnesota. My goal was to become a family therapist, and I wanted to work with teenagers. Soon, I got my chance. I had to volunteer a certain number of hours to complete my degree. I did an internship at The Bridge, an agency in Minneapolis that helped runaway and delinquent teenagers. The time I spent there was rewarding, and I was glad to be a part of it.

By then, Kim and Carl were teenagers, and they had done the usual things while in high school, like driving cars and going out at night. I couldn't complain; they were in a good circle of friends and both smart. But parents worry no matter how good their offspring are; we worry until they are tucked in their beds at night. Since Dallas's father had a problem with alcohol, I decided to take an evening class on alcoholism. I took notes, read a book on it, and learned what to look for in the behavior of youngsters as they became involved with peers who might use alcohol.

—⁓⁓⟡⟡⟡⟡⟡⟡⁓⁓—

Fast-forward to a cool morning in May 1986. The air was heady with the scent of blooming lilacs, and I was leaving the house for several hours. Dallas was at the office. Kim was at the University of Minnesota, where she was enrolled and lived on campus. Carl, still in high school, was just getting up from sleep. Although it was a weekday, he had begged for a mental health day the night before. I granted his request since he was an exceptional student.

I called Carl, "I won't be home for a while; will you be all right?"

He assured me he could fix his own lunch, so I headed out

the door.

I returned home at about four o'clock in the afternoon. As I approached our street, I couldn't believe what I saw. The block was cordoned off and swarming with fire trucks, police cars, television news vans, and an ambulance. Red and blue spinning lights added to the commotion. Coming closer, I was horrified to see flames shooting through the roof of our house. I parked the car and ran toward the scene. One frightening thing gripped my heart: my son is inside!

I stopped to catch my breath and was relieved when I saw Dallas and Kim holding our pets.

"Is Carl all right?" I said, gasping for air.

"Gerda, he's fine," Dallas quickly assured me. "He knew he couldn't do anything about the fire, so he kept his dental appointment." I took a deep breath and was numb. Thank God everyone is alive!

The agent from State Farm Insurance was there to go over some preliminary things. Surprisingly, I didn't mourn about the stuff inside the house. I was terribly thankful, though, when one of the firefighters came out with framed photographs from the walls and assured me that he had covered the mahogany furniture with a heavy tarp. "It can be restored," he told me.

In my shocked state, I recounted my life's tragedies: I've been bombed, I almost died from illness, I lost a mother, I was violated, I had a cruel father, and I was left alone to fight for my life. Dear God, I thought, why do I have to endure this too?

But God was not doing any explaining, at least not for the moment. We poked through the burned-out wreckage to remove whatever could be restored. Our clothing had to go to a special cleaner, and china and crystal were packed up. Everything else was thoroughly soaked and smelled like smoke. The fire started in the attic, where the wires had gotten too hot and were smoldering from one end to the other. All the ceilings had to be opened up, and the insulation was to be dropped to the floor. We floundered for hours in the knee-deep muck, trying to salvage what we could.

We rented an apartment for the four and a half months it took to rebuild our home. Rebuilding me took a little longer. I lost my books, papers, and tests from my college studies. I was overwhelmed by the idea of rebuilding the house from scratch. I couldn't entertain the notion of going back to school.

I prayed for guidance. "God, do you want me to quit?" I asked. The answer was in my head: You can help people without having a degree. The matter was settled; I quit my studies and focused on the life that was before me.

The date of the fire was May 6, 1986. Four days later, I received a letter telling me about my father's death.

The loss of my home was more devastating than the loss of my father.

CHAPTER 10
SURVIVING AND THRIVING

People often ask me why I came to this country. My answer is always the same: "I hated my father, and I hated Germany."

The other question I hear frequently is, "Do you feel home is in Germany or the United States?"

I have an answer to that question, too, and it comes easily. I point my finger at the sky and say, "I'm just passing through; I'm going to my heavenly home when God thinks that my work on earth is done." But there are many things I'd still like to do while I'm down here. God and I talk daily about my life, and I am sensitive to what He has in store for me. While writing my story, I have learned to be quiet so I can listen and seek His guidance. Life has been quite a rocky journey for me, but God has always carried me through. He let me see the beauty of Mr. Frost's magic on the cold windows when my sisters and I tried to get warm. He provided food to sustain us. He sheltered my family through the air raids. His loving arms were around me when our mother Dorothy died. He gave me courage, humor, and a strong survival instinct. I can honestly say God motivated my journey to America.

I sincerely hope my story will inspire readers to take God seriously and start the journey with Him sooner than I did. The only excuse I can offer is that my heart and mind were not emotionally healthy enough to let Jesus' love flow through my veins.

I still have a strong desire to help others in need. By serving others, I am serving Him. I underwent hospice training in Minnesota and Florida so I could ease people's final days on Earth. Three years ago, I took the intensive Stephen Ministry training to help bring God's love to people who are suffering. This ministry program provides laypeople with the knowledge and skills to be compassionate Christian caregivers.

Our daughter Kim is my friend and my inspiration. She and I have lengthy conversations about God and life. If I am angry with God for not making my life more harmonious, Kim reminds me, "Mother, you have to learn all these lessons so God can really use you!"

I used to be envious of American children who had a better life than I—proper parents, a religious upbringing, a good education, marrying, and having a healthy family. But I don't think that way anymore. I tend to count my blessings more these days.

Dallas and I moved to Venice, Florida, in 1998. We feel blessed to live in such a beautiful state. We don't mind the summer heat; it easily trumps the cold winters of Minnesota, where we lived for twenty-eight years. We have celebrated forty-plus wedding anniversaries. Our marriage has been complicated at times, but we loved each other enough to seek help when we needed it. When marriages are strained, a spouse will either run or stay. I am very fortunate that Dallas stayed and supported me through my journey.

I also feel blessed with a wonderful family. Raising our children might have been easier if I had learned Dr. Pilling's life-altering tools earlier. For a part of their lives, they had a mother gripped with chronic pain who couldn't cope with her repressed feelings. Our kids were fortunate to have parents who loved them and provided food, clothing, and a roof over their heads. But they also had many frills, including horseback riding lessons and piano lessons. I'm glad they had the extras, but I wish I had been able to give them more emotional support. They tell me I'm too hard on myself, but I do wish things could have been different.

For a long time, I couldn't work with children through my volunteering endeavors. It was just too difficult. But I've learned to do so with God's guidance. Now, when I talk to children, I'm not afraid to get down on my knees, look into their eyes, and try to understand their joys and hurts.

Our children have accomplished a lot in their lives thus far. Our daughter Kim lives in California with her husband, Robert St. Pierre. She works for Sage Publishing Co. It hasn't always been easy, but we are proud of what she has accomplished. Robert brings some special skills to our lives. He is a gifted animation artist. Of course, I can't talk about art, but we have a special relationship. We enjoyed her visits and wished California wasn't so far away.

Our son, Carl, is a neurology doctor who lives in Maine. It's sad that they live so far away. He married Kerry Breen in 1992, and they have two great sons, Tyler and Alec. We remember great times when they were little and visited us in Florida. Golf and tennis were our pastimes. They have completed their education and are working. Tyler works in advertising, and Alec has become a teacher. Again, our distances are too great. Fortunately, we have the technology.

It is my avid hope that I continue to have a special relationship with each of my family members for the rest of my life.

I'm sensitive to what my body is trying to tell me. If I find myself in physical distress—the usual aches and pains of an "older" person—I start with an over-the-counter pain pill. If my back hurts, I resort to my floor exercises to stretch and strengthen the muscles. If these initial steps don't relieve the pain, I see the internist or dentist. If everything checks out and I am still in pain, then I see my counselor, Dr. Christopher Cortman.

Finding the right counselor is half the battle. I've come to believe it can be as challenging as finding the proper mate. Dr. Cortman and I examine the cause and effect of my concerns. Once I think through my feelings and process them, I usually end up pain-free. So far, I have avoided heavy medications. Dr. Cortman is a godsend. His expertise, insights, and compassion helped keep me on the right course.

My hope and prayer is that my life experiences might encourage readers to connect with their hearts and learn to express their emotions. If you feel happy about something, let it be known. If someone upsets you, figure out a way to tell them without provoking anger or resentment. Through trial and error, I've learned when to speak out; after all, you don't want to get caught with your foot in your mouth. (I am a size 10, and it's painful to stick my foot in my mouth!)

Dr. Pilling encouraged me to let my feelings flow as easily as I breathed in and out. Don't let hurts fester—ask for forgiveness when you have wronged someone, forgive when you have been wronged, then move on.

I often wonder what would have happened to me if I had not met Dr. Pilling. His expertise in treating the body with the mind was instrumental in getting me well. I only can say that it was God's plan that I met him.

It took me many years to learn these lessons, but I'm happy with the results. I don't think I'd be living the active life I now have in my seventies. I play tennis and golf, volunteer at my church, and enjoy good health and happiness. I can't stress enough how important it is to deal with repressed emotions and how devastating to one's physical and emotional health it can be to ignore them.

QUICK FIXES

Healing from years of pent-up emotions associated with trauma, hardship, and loss is no quick or easy process, as I hope this book has made clear. However, not everyone has the luxury of entering a clinic for several weeks or seeing a therapist on an ongoing basis, and some people will resist this method of healing because of stigma, lack of faith in the effectiveness of treatment, or simply fear of what they might discover about themselves. Fortunately, there were some places along my journey where specific elements of the hurt could be healed by very direct interventions that didn't require long stints of expensive therapy. I call these my quick fixes, and I am sharing three of them here.

QUICK FIX #1: SMASHING TENNIS BALLS

I remember Dr. Pilling's words clearly. During one of his lectures, he explained that when feelings have been suppressed for a long time and are subsequently brought to the surface, strange things happen to our bodies. Your feelings resemble an ocean; sometimes, the waves are wild and uncontrollable, and other times, there is a smooth calm. The main objective counseled the doctor was to ride the waves instead of trying to tame them. Here's how I learned to ride the waves.

One day, when Dallas was at work and the kids were at school, I finished my household chores and enjoyed a rare time to reflect on things I hadn't thought about for a long time. I thought about how lucky my children were: they had loving parents, they had the opportunity to get an education, and they were well-fed. They never knew the despair that hunger could bring. Most importantly, they lived in a free country.

What a sharp contrast to my miserable youth! The more I

dwelled on my unhappy childhood, the more I wanted to cry.

I went into our bedroom and lay down on the bed. Hugging my pillow, I began to sob as I had never done before. The phone rang, but I ignored it. I was in no mood to talk to anybody. I don't remember how long I lay there before I fell into utter despair. Something had to give. I could take a Valium, pour myself a stiff drink, or find a place to hit some tennis balls. I discovered I could release a lot of anger when I smacked around a tennis ball; not only did it relieve my stress, it improved my game.

Smashing tennis balls was the smartest choice. I hurriedly dressed, grabbed my racquet, and gathered up a supply of tennis balls. I hoped the courts and the backboard were free at the local high school.

I was almost out the door when I heard the doorbell ring. I opened the door, and Sukran, a dear friend of mine, stood there. Her pretty face held her usual infectious smile. Born in Turkey, her exotic looks made me smile.

"Hi, my dear friend," I said, giving her a one-armed hug as I passed. She started to say something, but I interrupted her. "I can't talk right now; I'm on a mission. I'll call you this afternoon," I said, waving a farewell. I left her standing outside the front door and headed to my car.

On the way to the tennis courts, I succumbed to my old fears. Would I have been better off staying in Germany? What are my options now? I was tired of all the ghosts that haunted me, tired of the questions and doubts that plagued me, and tired of being tired.

Within ten minutes, I arrived at the tennis courts and was relieved to see that I was alone. I started hitting the balls, which was nice and easy at first. Then, I started striking the backboard with more force. Soon, I was sweating and breathing heavily. Not good enough. With every ounce of energy, I hit the ball harder.

I thought of every person who had hurt me: Hitler for starting the war, my father for despising my existence, my mother for dying too young. The balls were getting harder to hit, and my energy was diminishing, but I kept going. I thought of every person who ever said an unkind word to me. I was angry that I had allowed this to happen so many times without standing up for myself.

Maybe I should have been angry with God. "Why me? Why me? Why did I have to experience all that pain?" I screamed over and over again. Finally, I was so exhausted that I fell on the grass outside the courts and cried uncontrollably.

If anybody saw me like this, I bet I'd be carted away to the hospital. But not if it were Dr. Pilling. I think he would have been proud of me for getting in touch with my feelings and learning how to cope with the enormous turmoil swirling in my heart.

I finally got up, wiped my eyes, and dragged my body back to the car. I sniffled all the way home. I wandered to the backyard and felt guilty for being mad at God. I still couldn't let go of that anger.

Tante Erna had told me many times, "You can't go to heaven if you haven't forgiven others—you must forgive your father."

I realized that I had experienced the uncontrollable waves of emotion that Dr. Pilling warned me about. He was right; the waves were huge. In a way, it felt good to unleash my anger on everyone, including God. I knew that in time, I would be able to forgive them all, even if I couldn't do so yet.

Before the day was out, I was able to talk to God and thank Him for being with me through the terrible storm of my emotions. I humbly asked if He would forgive me for my negative thoughts.

But I sensed He would lead me to the still, calm waters.

Be patient with me; God is not finished with me yet.

QUICK FIX #2: SILENCING THE SIRENS

One winter morning, after the kids were grown and off to make their way in the world, I sat sipping my coffee, looking out at our backyard and savoring the moment. The pine trees looked spectacular, wrapped in a cloak of freshly fallen snow. One tree looked particularly handsome—it was the blue spruce Dallas had given me six years previously. He had planted it the first Mother's Day we celebrated in Minneapolis after moving from St. Louis, Missouri. It had been a joy to watch it grow through the years. It seemed like God Himself must have pruned its shape; it was that perfect.

I was reluctant to move, but I knew I had my daily chores to do, and I was planning to meet my friend Janice for lunch. Remember, a good German Hausfrau wouldn't think of leaving her home until it could pass a strict inspection. I kept an eye on the clock because I couldn't be late—punctuality is another habit I inherited from my German culture.

Humming and cleaning, I tackled my mundane tasks with a light heart. I don't remember why I was so happy; perhaps the peaceful scenery in our backyard soothed my soul, or perhaps I anticipated Janice's company.

I had first met her through our husbands, who both worked for IBM. Once I got to know her, she had a way of making me feel so comfortable. Janice liked to take things slowly; I didn't.

179

But we got along famously nevertheless. (There's a lot of truth to the notion that opposites attract.) Now, after casting a final glance around my apple-pie-order house, I was ready to drive over to meet her.

As soon as I stepped into the garage, the neighborhood siren went off. It must be one o'clock, I thought. I knew the city tested the sirens at that time on the first Wednesday of the month. The blaring sound brought back unpleasant memories of my life between three and seven years old, the time I lived in Wilhelmshaven during the war. Month after month, I had to tolerate the good city of Minneapolis's penchant for testing its equipment. The piercing, undulating sound triggered an uneasy feeling deep in my soul. That day, it was worse than usual. The intensity of my fear pushed me back inside. I called my friend.

"Janice, I can't leave the house right now. I'm so jittery and nervous." My mouth felt dry. My legs and arms were numb. "I'm so sorry; I have to cancel on you."

"That's too bad," she said, disappointment tingeing her voice. "I wish I could help you, Gerda." She knew a lot about human emotions, and I knew her intentions were sincere. "Are you sure you want to stay home? Why don't you come over so we can talk about it?"

"No, I can't," I said, "not today."

I told her I needed to figure out a way to calm myself, and then we hung up. As the anxiety mounted, I tried to listen to a gospel music tape. That usually helped, but not today. I began to get a little frantic, and then I remembered Dallas's employer provided a mental health hotline.

My hands shook as I dialed. Soon, a friendly voice listened to my plight. She gave me Jim Moore's telephone number and told me he was trained in "regressive imagery," a special method I didn't know existed. I made an appointment to see him in a couple of days. I felt calmer already, knowing there was someone who could help me with my anxiety.

On the day of my appointment, I sat in his waiting room. In spite of the comfortable surroundings, I was terrified. When my name was finally called, my heart started pounding so loudly that I had to wonder whether the other patients could hear it. The unknown can be very frightening.

As soon as I walked into his office, Jim Moore greeted me with open arms. "It's nice to meet you," he said in a warm and friendly voice.

His casual sweater and slacks emphasized his relaxed mood. Even his face looked warm and fuzzy.

After a few preliminary questions, Jim got to the point. "So, Gerda, you want to get rid of the anxiety you feel when you hear the sirens that remind you of the war in Germany?"

"Yes," I said, still nervous.

"No problem," he said, smiling through his bearded face. "We can do this quickly and easily." His approach was different from counseling. "I focus on minimizing the trigger points. You'll still hear the siren, but it will not affect you like it does now."

He seemed confident, but I was skeptical. "What?" I burst out. "You mean you can erase these memories in a few minutes? I've been dragging them around in my head for thirty-five years!"

He crossed his arms and nodded. "Yep," he answered. I took a deep breath and agreed, "Let's do it."

He directed me to a comfortable chair. We sat down and

began. "Close your eyes and imagine what it was like during the war.

Tell me what you see," Jim prompted. "Is it a photo or a movie?" "A movie."

"Is it black and white?"

"Yes, black and white," I said. "There weren't color films back then." I would have pictured those years in black and white anyway; there were so few flowers or pretty, bright dresses. What little color remained was turned dull by the cloudy and rainy weather.

"Take your time," his soothing voice continued, "and watch the whole movie. Let me know when you've reached the end."

An image formed behind my closed lids: I saw a little blonde Gerda listening to the radio. Suddenly, the music stopped, and the sirens started blasting away, warning us of another air raid that would soon take place in our city. Amid the shrieking sound, my sisters and I held our breath as we stared into each other's eyes. Is this the day we'll all be killed? We wondered.

Then I heard my mother tell Ilse to get Traute and me and get ready for the shelter. We scrambled around as we heard the planes approaching. We ran as fast as we could toward safety. This time, however, we were too late. The shelter's doors had closed, so we had to go back to our basement. There, we found several of our neighbors who also hadn't made it to the shelter on time either. The elderly Frau Olsen, who lived below us, frightened me with her moaning and groaning. I thought she might die right in front of me.

We never knew how long we would have to wait in terror; the air raids usually lasted several hours. Everyone breathed a

182

huge sigh of relief when the siren's more calming all-clear sounded, and we were allowed to return to our apartment. We had survived one more time.

I lifted my head and opened my eyes. "The movie is over."

Jim Moore said, "Gerda, let's rewind the movie. Do you know what an eight-millimeter movie sounds like when it gets rewound?"

"Yes," I nodded.

"Well, we're going to rewind it right now. Then it will be erased!" I closed my eyes and "rewound" the movie in my head.

"Let's practice this a few times. We'll talk about it again when you hear the siren."

I shrugged my shoulders, doubtful this would help, but I repeated the exercise with him.

When we finished "erasing" my memories, Jim asked, "Is there anything else that bothers you?" His smile was so genuine I started to cry. "What are those tears about?"

I realized I had other unresolved issues lurking in my past. "I wish I could forget the horrible way my father treated me. He made me feel inferior."

I told him that when I was ten, he was released from the Russian prisoner-of-war camp. The abuse started then and continued until I was sixteen.

"Tell me more," Jim said.

"I hated him! I hated Germany!" I clenched my hands into tight fists. "That's why I came to the United States. I could never do anything right for him. My older sisters, Ilse and

183

Traute, were treated the same way, yet he didn't have the same effect on them." I sighed. "Maybe I'm too sensitive?"

"Maybe so," he replied. "Are there times when you feel inadequate?" "Yes, I feel that way often, especially at meetings, or volunteering at my church … any type of social setting." I tried to calm my breathing. "I think about myself negatively—all the time," I explained how sharp and demanding my father was—the perennially disapproving tone of his voice still haunted me. Constantly barking orders, he expected my sisters and me to drop everything to satisfy his demands. If we disobeyed him, the stare of those cold blue eyes would stab us with contempt and disgust. He was truly a self-centered tyrant. How often we wished he had never returned from Russia. At least the years he was held prisoner, from 1945 until 1948, our lives were free of his cruel behavior.

Jim nodded, and then he said softly, "Let's work to get rid of those terrible memories too."

"Oh, am I going to imagine another movie?" I asked.

"No, but the technique is very similar."

If this type of therapy is so successful, I wondered, why isn't it used all the time?

He seemed to read my mind and just shrugged his shoulders. "Now, Gerda, let's erase those nasty blue eyes."

I was still apprehensive about his methodology, but I was also determined to keep an open mind.

First, Jim asked me if I had a photograph of my father at home. I did. It was hidden in the bottom of my closet—I'd never felt the need to hang it up.

"When you go home," he continued, "I want you to look at your father's picture. Then walk away from it slowly." He

184

held up his hands, palms facing each other, about a foot apart. "Watch the image getting smaller and smaller." Inch by inch, he opened the gap between his hands until his arms were outstretched. "Do this exercise several times. Eventually, you won't see him in the same way." He nodded his conviction. "I also want you to think about yourself as a grown-up. Who are you? What makes you special? Where do you get your support from?" Not accustomed to thinking of myself as special, I had to ponder all those questions for a moment. My husband thinks I'm a great wife and a wonderful mother. He considers me a wonderful, caring, and loving person. My friends often tell me how much they love my humor and kindness. My then-twelve-year-old daughter Kim had commented that I was smarter than many of her friends' mothers. I volunteered at a hospice where patients and nurses appreciated the loving care I dispensed.

Now that I examined my present life, I realized I had much to be thankful for.

"Now," Jim said, "I'd like you to close your eyes again. Imagine the wise, kind, and loving woman you are today soothing that little Gerda who so desperately needed comfort. The adult Gerda knows all the hurt inside the little Gerda; she can take care of her better than anyone else." I felt the tears roll slowly down my face. Silently, I mourned for the childhood I never had. Up until this point in my life, I never realized how alone I felt as a child and how much I missed having a normal childhood.

My eyes were still shut when I felt him place a teddy bear in my arms.

"Let the big Gerda comfort the little one," he said.

I was uncomfortable with his method—it made me feel a little weird at first. Gradually, I felt a little more comfortable hugging the little Gerda. With a deep sigh, I asked, "Can we stop now? It's getting overwhelming."

He encouraged me to continue for a while, just to let the peacefulness sink in.

Right after the exercise concluded, I asked, "So, when will I know if this worked?"

"Gerda, you have to trust me! Let's make an appointment after next month's siren episode, and we'll talk about it then. Remember to practice the imagery techniques at home— they'll work anywhere." He exuded so much confidence that I had to trust him even though I still had doubts. I have nothing to lose, I thought. "I'm counting on you," I said as I left his office.

When I got home, I immediately called Janice and told her about my visit with Jim Moore. "I'm amazed how much better I feel," I told her. "But I'm still skeptical."

"I'm sure you are," Janice replied. "But let's just wait and see what happens."

We spoke a little longer about my visit, and she reassured me that I had made the right decision to seek help.

Later that day, I dug out my father's photo from the closet. I placed it on the dresser. Slowly, I backed away from his image, as Jim Moore had suggested. As his face got smaller, I realized he seemed to have less power over me. I even began to feel sorry for him. Maybe he had a lousy childhood, too; maybe he didn't know how to be a kind and supportive father. Feeling some compassion for the father I had only hated before—that was definitely progress. Although I wasn't ready yet to hang up his picture on the living room wall, I knew I had something here that I could really work with.

The first Wednesday of the month loomed darkly. When I heard the siren, I didn't even remember where I was. I checked my watch, satisfied it was one o'clock. My mind filled up with memories of surviving the German war. I understood why I had to grieve for the child who endured the constant fear of death.

I also thought about Dr. Pilling—my hero—the man who cared for me a few years ago at the pain and rehabilitation center. He always stressed the importance of letting things go and connecting the mind with the heart.

"Listen to your heart and your mind when you make decisions," he said.

I've tried to live up to that good advice, but it has been a slow process. I'm happy to report that my awareness about feelings has sharpened. Little by little, I go forward.

For the next few months, I allowed my heart—and my head—to process a lot of information. After that, whenever I heard the sirens, I glanced at my watch and smiled.

QUICK FIX #3: TALKING TO THE DEAD

Some days, when I looked out the window, the flowers didn't seem to sparkle just right, and the overcast sky weighed heavily on my psyche. It was disturbing to be so easily engulfed by my gloomy past—again and again. Would I ever be able to break free from that depressing merry-go-round?

One afternoon, as I wrestled with another episode of the blues, I began to ponder the death of both my mother, who passed away when she was forty, and my mother-in-law, who lived until she was fifty- eight. An all-too-familiar sense of loneliness gripped my heart; the losses were overwhelming. My sad thoughts wandered back to my family in Germany. I still missed them. Maybe I would have been happier if I had never come to America. Stop it, Gerda, I admonished myself. You're making yourself crazy! What more could I want? I had a wonderful, loving husband and two great kids. Now, I was rationalizing my happiness—trying to convince myself that I was content when I wasn't—something Dr. Pilling frowned upon.

"Don't deny those feelings," he had counseled, "process them!" Denny, another therapist who worked with me regularly at Dr. Pilling's clinic, once gave a lecture about what unprocessed feelings can do to your body. He used this analogy: unprocessed emotions are like garbage that the body collects. Eventually, the trash can overflows, and soon, the whole house starts to smell.

I began to realize that I had never processed my grief from the deaths of these two women who had been so important in my life; instead, I searched for maternal replacements.

The first replacement was a woman named Dorothy Nieman, whom I initially met at an international tea social. We took to one another right away, and soon, our friendship expanded to include Dallas and Dorothy's husband, Chuck. The four of us socialized together a lot, and we became close—so close, in fact, that Dorothy named us as her healthcare surrogates in her living will.

She had a beautiful red glass swan displayed on her grand piano. I often admired it, and one day Dorothy confided to me, "Gerda, I wrote your name on the bottom of the swan. I want you to have something to remember me by when I'm gone."

"That's nice," I said, shrugging off the unpleasant discussion about her death.

When she died unexpectedly, I felt the loss, but I didn't

really process the grief.

Later, I befriended a neighbor, Bobbie Morck, a recent widow. At one point, she suffered a broken wrist, and I volunteered to take her to the hairdresser and the grocery store once a week until she could drive again. We bonded during her recovery period and became fast friends. Through the years, she grew to be a part of our family, often spending holidays and birthdays with us. Then she died, too. Another loss, another pocketful of grief to tuck away.

I became saddled with a lot of deaths that I just couldn't process. As with much of my unfinished business of the past, I felt an overwhelming sadness followed by anger. Why couldn't I grieve properly for all those people who had died? I could barely think about death at all.

I wondered if Jim Moore could give me guidance. Through his regressive imagery technique, I had been able to dismiss the hurtful memories of my father, and I no longer cowered at the sound of sirens. Perhaps he would come through for me again. I made the appointment, and soon, I was sitting with him in his office. He described a method I could use to encourage the grieving process. I returned home, eager to begin.

The next morning, when everyone had left for school or work, I walked into the guest room to surround myself with the memories of all the ladies I lost. I placed pictures of my mother and mother-in-law on the dresser. I thought about my dear friend Dorothy Nieman and brought the glass swan into the room. I sat on the bed and regarded the beautiful antique furniture Bobbie Morck's family had given us. In essence, the room was a shrine to all the older ladies I had clung to yet couldn't grieve for. I called each one by name in the order they came into my life, just like Jim Moore taught me.

First, my mother. I found myself shouting at her black-and-white image, expressing things I'd held back for years. I confronted her emotional withdrawal and her inability to nurture and comfort me when I was a child and needed it so desperately. As I released my anger, an outburst of tears erupted that I couldn't begin to control. At one point, I shouted out questions to God, "Why did I have to endure so much sadness during my childhood? What did I ever do to deserve this?" The silence grew; I knew I wouldn't get any answers until He called me home.

Next, I turned to Dorothy Robinson's photograph. As I gazed into her eyes, I spoke to her as if she were alive and right there in front of me. "Why, why, did you leave me just when I had found you?" I felt especially sad since my mother-in-law was so kind and supportive— the first time I experienced such a nurturing relationship. We shared our joys and sorrows. "You are such a dear person," I continued, "and I'm so sorry you won't be in our lives." I addressed God once again. "Why did you have to take her from me?" Again, I knew there would be no ready answers.

I remember one night when I was visiting her just before she died. She held my hand and said, "Gerda, will you apologize to your aunt for me? I'm sorry I won't be here to meet her. I was looking forward to meeting someone from your family." As she clung to me, she described the beautiful things she saw: the billowing white curtains and an abundance of colorful flowers. "I wish you could see this. It's so pretty here." I was frightened when she continued, "Please don't go home yet, and … don't turn on the light."

I wanted to stay, but I had a babysitter who needed to get home. The next time I saw her, she was in the Intensive Care Unit at St. John's Hospital in St. Louis. I stood by her bed and gazed down at the woman who had given me so much love and respect. Her husband, Carl, was an alcoholic, and I thought God should take him instead of her. It was an unkind thought, and I felt guilty. (Guilty feelings came so easily.) Little did I know that Dorothy would be gone within two days.

As my eyes passed over the objects on my little shrine, I remembered I had two more people to acknowledge. I was exhausted from crying and reliving the memories of my mother and mother-in-law, but I forced myself to continue.

Dorothy Nieman, the original owner of the exquisite red glass swan, was a wonderful friend. She took me to the Minneapolis Women's Club, where we shared delicious lunches while we listened to interesting and informative guest speakers. While I mingled with the members of the club, I felt important and confident.

As I caressed the smooth surface of the glass swan, I told my dear friend that I was all right and that I didn't need important people to bolster my self-esteem.

The last person I needed to connect with was Bobbie Morck, my neighbor. I admired the beautiful dark mahogany furniture her family gave me. She had no children to claim it, and her husband Otto had already passed on when I first met her.

Bobbie's life wasn't a happy one. Apparently, Otto was mean. He also refused to let her go to work, which was a shame—she was such a talented artist. In fact, she had given me the first choice of some of her earliest greeting card designs. They were displayed in this room along with her hundred-year-old furniture.

In the quietness of the room, I thanked Bobbie for her friendship. She was eighty-eight when she died, and I had looked after her for more than twelve years. I was able to let her go, glad I could bring a little sunshine to the cloudy days of her life.

Now that I had given each of these ladies a final, proper farewell, I felt drained; however, the relief was enormous. Eventually, I was able to include my mother's picture in our living room. I learned another valuable lesson: the more attention we devote to our emotions, the more clarity we gain in our lives.

STEPS TO A HAPPIER LIFE

These steps helped build happiness in my life. I hope they make a difference in yours.

- Make time to connect with people who are important to you. A few moments of quality time are worth more than gold.
- Validate and empathize. Everybody likes to be heard and understood. It is important that we focus on what one another is actually saying instead of any story we may be constructing in our heads. It takes time and awareness to listen creatively.
- Try not to store feelings. It is easier to talk about disturbances (or happiness) when it occurs. Process your feelings daily so they don't build up. You will avoid explosions.
- Be generous with honest feedback, and don't forget to lead with a positive comment. Words are powerful; they can make or break a person.
- Take time for yourself. Nobody can make you happy; that is your job. If you love yourself, then you have love to give.
- Seek support in your journey. Some counseling services may be financially out of reach, but churches and government services are available and can be a great help.
- Teach children early by giving feelings their proper names: anger, fear, worry, grief, joy, sadness, guilt, and jealousy. Help children express themselves. They do not have the vocabulary. Rephrase and ask questions.
- Try to understand people who are going through difficult times. Look for and acknowledge positive changes. Everyone has value and needs love and acceptance.

- Listen and talk with your eyes. What does that mean exactly? Here's a story to illustrate: a five-year-old girl was in the kitchen with her busy mother. The little girl complained, "You're not listening to me!"

"Yes, I am," said the mother.

"No, Mom, you're not. Put me on the counter," instructed the little girl. The mother complied. The little girl placed her hands on her mother's cheeks and said, "Mother, I want you to listen with your eyes!"

ACKNOWLEDGMENTS

There were many people who enabled me to write my story, but foremost is my hero—Dr. Loran Pilling. His guidance pulled me up from the deepest valley and placed me on a mountaintop. He restored my health. Dallas and I have no words to adequately describe the great gift he gave us.

Bill and Phyllis Cooper from Edina, Minnesota, were the first ones to recognize that I had a story to tell. Bill developed an outline to get me started. Sadly, Bill passed away, but Phyllis is eager to read these pages. I thank them both for their encouragement and persistence in motivating me.

The Jacaranda Writers Group at our local library in Venice, Florida, was instrumental in my commitment to write this book. Louise Reiter, co-founder and mentor of the group, is a former editor for The Palm Beach Post. On the first and third Tuesdays of the month during 2011, I submitted drafts of my chapters. I listened and learned from her, as well as the other group members. Because of their enthusiastic support, I took my writing more seriously. Louise also rewrote much of the material here. I gave her plenty of words, and she had the expertise to rearrange them so eloquently. Thank you, Louise, for meeting my impossible deadline!

I want to thank my husband, Dallas, who supported me in every way, including capturing my handwritten memoir scribbling onto the computer. His love, patience, persistence, and guidance have been overwhelming. Without him, I would have never gone through the process. His was truly a labor of love.

Our daughter Kim, who was a journalism major at the University of Minnesota, started as an editor at SAGE Publications. Twenty years later, she is the Director of

Organizational Development. I can't say enough about our Kim; she has been and is still my motivator and cheerleader. She knew that at the guru.com website, I could find the developmental and organizational help I needed.

Thanks to the vision of Bonnie Lynch of Karuna Solutions Consulting. I hired her to organize and develop some of my material. We worked closely during 2012, in person and by phone and e-mail. It has been a pleasure working with her.

My acknowledgments would not be complete without the mention of therapist Dr. Christopher Cortman of Venice, Florida. He came highly recommended by our long-time internist, Dr. Jack Rodman. Dr. Cortman is a highly sought-after speaker. With his many years of experience in the field of psychology, he addresses mental health topics with knowledge, humor, and down-to-earth solutions. He co-authored the book Your Mind: An Owner's Manual for a Better Life (Career Press, 2009). He also helped me adjust to the Florida country club lifestyle and to face my past with an open mind and a loving heart. I recommend him regularly to friends who seek help.

I think it's super that there are so many caring and competent people out there to help with our problems. Remember to embrace their offering of help and deal with it. My new motto is "Dealing Is Healing."